Foreword By
Emmanuel Dei-Tumi
(CEO, Future Leaders Group)

Fulfilling YOUR DESTINY

Principles for Maximising your Life

JOSEPH BOATENG

FULFILLING YOUR DESTINY©
Copyright © 2016 JOSEPH BOATENG.
ISBN: 978-9988-2-3368-6

All rights reserved. Under international copyright Law, no part of this publication may be reproduced, stored, or transmitted by any means without written permission from the publisher.

JOEBOAT MINISTRIES INTERNATIONAL
P. O. Box 3199, Accra, Ghana
Cell Phone: +233 249 966 449 / 509 178 077
E-mail: joeboat250@yahoo.com
Skype name: joeboat250

Edited by:
Conrad Kakraba (Former Newscaster/Editor, GTV)
P.O.Box LG 925, Legon, Accra
Tel: +233 209 011 405
Email: kakraba2008@yahoo.com
Facebook: Conrad Kakraba

Published by:
Joeboat Publication Inc.
A division of Joeboat Ministries International.

Cover Design & Page Layout
Indes Procom Limited
www.indesprocom.com

TABLE OF CONTENT

Dedication	iv
Acknowledgement	v
Vision & Mision Statements	vii
Foreword	viii
Introduction	x
From The Authors Desk	xv

Chapter 1
YOUR GIFTS AND TALENTS — 1

Chapter 2
GOD'S PURPOSE FOR YOUR GIFTS AND TALENTS — 31

Chapter 3
DEVELOP YOUR GIFTS AND TALENTS — 77

Chapter 4
GOD'S WAY OF FULFILLING YOUR DESTINY — 113

Chapter 5
IF YOU ARE WILLING AND OBEDIENT — 161

DEDICATION

I dedicate this book to my precious mother for being a virtuous woman and the kind of mother everyone will love to have. Her life is an example of a woman who maximized her potentials and allowed her life to be a blessing in the lives of many other people.

Auntie Mansa (as she is affectionately called), may the Good Lord reward you for all your labors. Even in your old age (85yrs) you are still making a difference in the lives of people. You keep saying that you want your life to make a difference in the lives of people and that is exactly what your life has become. Indeed you are a blessing to mankind.

ACKNOWLEDGEMENT

I want to first of all acknowledge and thank the Almighty God for seeing me fit to be called into his work. But for his grace I would not be doing his work. I thank him for his mighty power which is greatly at work in me both to will and to do of his good pleasure (purpose).

Many thanks to my Parents and the late Mr. Kofi Gyeni-Boateng (Snr. brother –RIP), for sponsoring my education. My ability to read and write is because of them.

Many thanks also to Mr. Emmanuel Dei-Tumi, who is one of two pioneers of the motivational speaking industry in Ghana and has developed into one of the nation's foremost authorities in unearthing and tapping into human potential. I want to appreciate him for his willingness and commitment to foreword this book. His rich experience as a motivational speaker, a youth development practitioner, an author, a training consultant, an entrepreneur, a philanthropist and a radio and television personality, has been a great source of encouragement.

I also want to acknowledge Mr. Conrad Kakraba (Former Newscaster/Editor, GTV) for the excellent editing he did on this book. I am grateful for his immense contribution.

The Bible says that, "There is a friend that sticks closer than a brother." This is so true of Pastor Praise Adu-Gyamfi. He is a true friend I call a covenant brother. The impact of his friend-ship on my life cannot be over emphasized.

VISION STATEMENT

- To Raise for God true worshipers who will worship Him in spirit and in truth.
- To preach about the liberation of women.
- To bring revival to people and churches.

MISSION STATEMENT

- Teaching God's people how to get closer to God with all of their spirit, soul and body.
- Teaching women the right understanding of their God given roles.
- Manifesting the awesome presence of God.

RESULT STATEMENT

- A people dedicated to God in worship - thus moving God's people from self-centeredness to God-centeredness.
- The empowerment of women and the education of men to form a strong bond of oneness in fulfilling divine destiny (a common destiny).
- Out of the belly will flow rivers of living waters which will bring great spiritual, physical, emotional, psychological and mental healing to people.

FOREWORD

In Jeremiah 1:5 God specifically made it known to the prophet Jeremiah that, "Before I formed you in the womb I knew you, before you were born I sanctified you; and I ordained you a prophet to the nation." Similarly, God made His purpose concerning Joseph, Moses, Paul and our Lord Jesus Christ known to each of them.

Personally, on the 23rd of October 1997, in a hotel room in Ghana, the Lord revealed my purpose to me in what could be summed up like:

"I am sending you to teach my people how to discover their potentials and empower them with the necessary strategies to maximize their level of success".

Knowing your purpose in life is paramount to the fulfilment of your destiny. Your destiny is your expected end. However, your destiny is not yours to decide; rather it's meant to be discovered.

As you read through this book, you will gain a deeper insight into your destiny and how to fulfil it. You will also know the essence of your gifts and talents in relation to your destiny. Since you cannot fulfil your destiny without adequate preparation, this book will also share with you strategies on how to prepare sufficiently in order to accomplish your purpose.

The principles espoused in this book, *Fulfilling Your Destiny* by Joseph Boateng is simple and easy to read and understand. All you need is to practice constantly these principles and watch yourself fulfil your great destiny and take your rightful place among humanity.

I highly recommend this book for all who desire to make great impact in this world, and those struggling to discover their destiny.

Emmanuel Dei-Tumi
CEO, Future Leaders Group.

INTRODUCTION

People have erroneously thought that fate and destiny are synonymous. According to them, destiny is wherever you find yourself. But this is not so. Wherever you find yourself in life is fate, not destiny.

Destiny is about driving towards a definite goal or destination. Unlike fate, where you accept whatever comes your way, destiny is based on the knowledge of your purpose on the earth. Your destiny is delivered to you by God. God hasn't created you a purposeless being on the earth; you are a creature of purpose, and have a clearly defined destiny. Hear what He says about you in **Jeremiah 29:11: For I know the thoughts that I think toward you, says the Lord, thoughts of peace, and not of evil, to give you an expected end.**

God has an expected end for you; that is your destiny. But it is your responsibility to discover it through a search. Discovering your destiny in life begins with your identifying your purpose. To be purposeless is to be powerless, because energy is only released when you are driving towards a well-defined goal or destination. Nothing produces energy like purpose or goal. That is why a day without any set goal is a very tiring one. Destiny begins with an identified purpose; men of purpose are men of power. Martin Luther King Jnr. Said, "**If a man has no purpose for living, he is not fit to live.**" When a man has no purpose in life, then life itself remains a burden to him, because he is a burden to existence.

There are some secrets about you that nobody knows. Information about who you really are and why you are on this earth is not known by anybody, not even your parents. No natural eye, neither ear nor the heart of man knows about it. The manufacturer (God) of your life is the only one who has this information about you and does not reveal it to anybody else except you alone. This secret information are what truly define who you really are, and what your mission on this earth is all about and until it is revealed to you, any other information concerning you from any other source is a lie. The manufacturer (God) is the one who has the details of the information concerning your life and if there is anything you must do, then it is to seek Him for that information (revelation).

God is unfolding the stories of men in these last days. Men are being opened up to the detailed plan of God for their lives. No longer will man walk in darkness concerning who he truly is, and why he is here on this earth. The destinies of men (mankind) are being opened up to them. The volume of the things written concerning the destinies of men are being opened up to them by the Spirit of God. **Men, hear the call of God for this hour. Men, get ready!** For God is opening you up to the very details of your life. You will no longer waste your life on this earth. For you shall be like Paul who said, **"I have fought a good fight, I have run the race and I have finished my course"**.

I see frustrations and failures in the lives of people coming to an end, because I see men of all races embracing the details of their God given destinies, especially Africans. Now, the hour for Africa has come. Many Africans who for lack of understanding of their proper placement in destiny - who were subjected to all forms of frustrations and failures, are now receiving a fresh baptism of revelation of their proper placement in God's plan. Men shall rise up boldly because they will know who they are as far as God's plan for them is concerned and what they are sent on this earth to do. Uncertainty and confusion are coming to an end, especially in Africa.

The Lord of hosts is gathering his own army on the continent of Africa. There will be more Africans in His army because they have not yet experienced the freedom that comes as a result of **proper placement in destiny**. It's time that people discover their purpose for coming to this earth. Without purpose, then you have not really started living. Find out why God brought you to this earth. Until you find out this important answer, your life has not yet began - you are just existing.

What are the gifts and talents that you have been endowed with for your life purposes? Do you know what your life purposes are? How do you even prepare yourself for the assignment you are uniquely called for? What and when is the best way to fulfill your destiny in life? Your destiny is a combination of your gifts and talents and the specific assignments they are meant to accomplish on earth.

The discovery of your gifts and talents is the sure start for the fulfillment of your destiny. In addition to the gifts and talents come special responsibilities for developing and managing them for a **God-ordained purpose.** This is a process you must be willing to go through for the fulfillment of your God-ordained destiny. You must be willing to discover your gifts and talents, and also be willing to find out the purpose for which God gave them to you.

As we all know, only few materials can be used in their raw and natural state unless they have been processed or developed. In the same way, your gifts and talents cannot be effective until they are well developed. This will require a lot of effort on your part for you to be ready to fulfill your destiny. Until our gifts and talents are well developed, they cannot be effective in accomplishing their purposes. It is after your gifts and talents are developed that you can then think of how best you can now accomplish the purposes for which they were given. It is my prayer that God will give you the grace to be able to discover the hidden gifts and talents in you and also have the grace to maximize them for your profiting and the world around you. It isn't enough to have potentials; you must also maximize them for the benefit of mankind.

The purpose of this book is to make you examine and challenge the many opinions you have lived under for years. My deepest desire is to release in you the courage to pursue the potential that lies deep within you, to tap into the reserve of creativity yet unseen by your peers and generations to come. You must promise yourself that you will read this book again and again until the principles and truth in it become a natural part of your thinking and you come to the awareness that understanding and releasing your gifts and talents is simply becoming yourself as God our creator originally intended. It's worth knowing that, your destiny is a combination of your gifts and talents and the specific assignments they are meant to accomplish on earth.

Remember nothing is impossible to him who believes. Enjoy the journey through this timely book. May God reward your diligence.

Joseph Boateng
Joeboat Ministry Int.

YOUR GREATEST GIFT IS TODAY

"The secret to life is effective management of time and change. The principal key to management of time and change is planning. Planning is the most important principle of success in life. The only regulator of time and change is planning"

— *Myles Munroe* —

If you want tomorrow to be great and wonderful for you, then start doing great and wonderful things today. The greatest gift God can ever give to you is today (24hours). This is the day that the LORD has made therefore rejoice and be glad in it (be up and doing). Do you know that one of the most dangerous things in life is wasting time? Once you've lost time, it's gone forever. So the best thing to do with time is to use it in a way that will bring the greatest results. The best way and the only way to use time effectively is to do what you are supposed to do when you are supposed to do it. Effectiveness does not mean just doing good things (human plans) but rather doing the right things (divine plans).

You wake up in the morning, and lo! Your purse is wonderfully filled with twenty-four hours of the unmanufactured tissue of the universe of your life! It is yours. It is the most precious possession. A highly singular commodity, showered upon you in a manner as singular as the commodity itself! No one can take it from you. It is "unstealable". And no one receives either more or less. You must therefore ask yourself, **"What am I going to do with the gift of today that God has given to me?"** That is, the 24hours of each day. Are you investing or wasting it?

> *The secret to life is effective management of time and change. The principal key to management of time and change is planning. Planning is the most important principle of success in life. The only regulator of time and change is planning.*

You have to live on this twenty-four hours of daily time. Out of it you have to spin health, pleasure, money, content, respect, and the discovery of who you are. Its right use, its most effective use, is a matter of the highest urgency and of the most thrilling actuality. All depends on that. Many do not teach or talk about, *"How to live on a given income of time,"* but instead on *"How to live on a given income of money"*!

Money is far more common than time in our day. The misuse of anything as precious as time, should be a crime. If someone steals your car, it would be an inconvenience but not a tragedy because you can easily acquire another. If someone snatches your wallet, it would be an annoyance but few phone calls would salvage the majority of your concerns. But who can you call if you suffer the loss of time - and not just time, but your time? But if I may ask, "O man, what have you done with your life? What are you doing with your youth?" You have to make every time count if you are ever to fulfill your purpose.

> *You have to make your life count if you are ever to fulfill your purpose.*

The secret to life is **effective management of time and change.** The Principal **Key to management of time and change is planning. Planning** is the most important Principle of Success in Life. The only regulator of **time** and **change** is **planning.** Planning coupled with hard work (action) is all you need to start from where you are towards where you want to get to in life. Remember, anything the **mind** can conceive the **hand** can achieve. **(Proverbs 21:5)**

> *If you want tomorrow to be great and wonderful for you, then start doing great and wonderful things TODAY.*

Without the opportunity of today you don't have tomorrow, so why then do you worry about tomorrow when you have been given today? "Don't worry about tomorrow, for tomorrow will care for its own worries. Today's trouble is enough for today"- Matthew 6:34. God gave you today so that your tomorrow can be colorful; therefore don't waste today. Spend today meaningfully, purposefully, productively and creatively. In fact spend each day wisely. The book of Ephesians says that, Therefore be careful how you walk, not as unwise people but as wise, **MAKING THE MOST OF YOUR TIME**, because the days are evil (Ephesians 5:15-16). Any wasted day called today is a wasted tomorrow and any wasted tomorrow is a lost destiny. You must live your life on purpose and not leave it to chance. For anyone who leaves his or her life to chance has no chance and is bound to face difficult days (evil days). There must be purpose in every step you take. There must be a conscious effort to utilize each day fully without wasting it.

You must spend TODAY meaningfully, purposefully, productively and creatively

A wasted time, called today, will lead to an unproductive life, tomorrow. How you spend today will determine what comes to you tomorrow. What you are today is the result of what you did with your time yesterday. Time does not wait for you. Time lost can never be regained. Once this minute passes you by, you can't get it back. Hence it is imperative that something useful is done with the time. Look at what the Bible says in the book of proverbs. **"The lazy man does not plow after the autumn, so he begs during harvest and has nothing." (Proverbs 20:4).**

Today's investments are tomorrow's returns. Therefore invest today wisely. If you do not plow today, you will then beg tomorrow. Whoever squanders and misuses today, will surely be a slave or a servant tomorrow. Don't worry about your tomorrow, but rather do something wisely about your today; for what happens to you tomorrow depends on what you do today. If you do nothing today you cannot expect to receive anything tomorrow. Don't focus your energies on where you must be tomorrow, but rather concentrate on what is required to be done today. *Your future is a direct derivative of the plans you place in motion today.*

> *A wasted time, called TODAY, is a wasted tomorrow and any wasted tomorrow is a lost destiny.*

Disciplined focus on what you do today is what distinguishes those who make things happen from those that watch things happen. Stay blessed as you make each day count! Your glorious destiny depends on it. The Bible says that, TODAY if you hear his voice, harden not your heart. Life is all about what you do TODAY. Make that decision today and get moving today, for the whole world is waiting for your manifestation (Romans 8: 19).

TODAY'S investments are tomorrow's returns. This is very important

From The Author's Desk.

It is chiefly through books that we enjoy intercourse with superior minds... In the best books, great men talk to us, give us their most precious thoughts, and pour their souls into ours. God be thanked for books. They are the voices of the near, distant and the dead, and make us heirs of the spiritual life of past ages. Books are true levelers. They give to all, who will faithfully use them, the society, the spiritual presence, of the best and greatest of our race.

— *William Ellery Channing*

CHAPTER ONE

YOUR GIFTS AND TALENTS

"The man who is born with a gift and talent, which he is meant to use, finds his greatest happiness in using it"

– Johann Von Goethe –

Everyone has things that come easily to them. Things they do that are almost effortless yet create amazing results. The tasks you excel at reveal your natural gifts and talents. They describe what you are naturally great at doing. If you develop them and put them to work, you have the beginning of a great career or business or calling.

> *If you develop them and put them to work, you have the beginning of a great career or business or calling.*

The gifts and talents God gave you are your keys to success. Gifts and Talents are different from skills, in that they tend to be innate rather than learned. They are given to you from birth. You are born with them. Once found, they can be nurtured and developed, but finding them is the challenge for most people. It's partly a process of self-observation and being honest with yourself. The rest is through learning and practice. Gifts and Talents can come in many varieties. They may be artistic or technical, mental or physical, inwardly or outwardly directed. These gifts and talents will always be your own, part of what makes you "you".

WHAT MAKES YOU UNIQUE?

Do you wonder what makes you different from everyone else? Are you looking for an answer to "what makes you special and unique?" That which is more meaningful than just your FINGERPRINTS or your DNA? Understanding how each of us is unique is an essential part of questioning who we are and why we exist. To help you find an answer to this ancient question, I offer a new way of looking at things. One important truth is that, every living thing that God created was blessed with potential and that includes you.

POTENTIAL: Is dormant gifts, hidden talents, untapped strength, unexposed ability, and unused power.

TALENT/GIFTS: It is a natural ability for being good at a particular activity without any formal training.

You must note that, your gifts and talents describe in detail who you are. Moreover, that description is so detailed it defines how you are unique on this planet. Just as no twins are alike, you are like no one else. You are the only one who has your exact combination of potentials. You are extraordinary; there has never been anyone exactly like you in all the history of mankind on earth. You are no more than or less than anybody else is. You are only less than your full potential, and thus capable of becoming more than you are now. You are capable of much more than you are presently thinking, imagining, doing or being.

> *You are only less than your full potential, and thus capable of much more than you are presently doing.*

Our potential is a paradox that makes us at the same time both a part of the human family and unique within that family. We are united by our having gifts, talents, life callings and dreams of an extraordinary life. However, we are each unique because all of our gifts, talents, life callings and dreams are different. In my experience, everyone has at least 5 to 10 uncommon gifts or talents they can excel at. For if, you are a truly unique expression of life, then only you have the gifts, and talents or potential to excel at the unique tasks, which define your destiny and your life calling. No one can fulfill the life calling you are uniquely qualified for. If you do not do it, it will go undone, or done by someone else in a very different way.

Do you not realize that all of your ability, talents and resources have been predetermined so you can accomplish your purpose? They are like a toolbox of equipment and accessories that are

God-given for your use to attain what He has determined. In other words, you are built to do what He has called you to accomplish.

> *"You are the only one who has your exact combination of potentials to excel at the unique tasks, which define your destiny and your life calling".*

Your special talents and gifts might turn toward sports, writing, art, sewing, pottery, communication, singing, dancing, teaching,— the list is endless. It may be a business talent or strength of character. But my bet is – you don't recognize your own special gifts and talents. That special thing you do, which is so "easy," so you assume anyone could do it! And since our natural talents are so easy to "put down," or overlook, often that's just what happens in early life. We often say they are our hobbies. They are the things we do for the fun of it, just for our satisfaction. But we never get down to committing our lives to them. Along life's journey we drop them to do something "serious".

> *You are extraordinary; there has never been anyone exactly like you in all the history of mankind on earth. No one can fulfill the life calling you are uniquely qualified for. If you do not do it, it will go undone, or done by someone else in a very different way.*

The artistic child is told to "forget drawing" and study something "serious". Or the young avid reader on his way to becoming a gifted writer is told to "get his head out of books" and go play with the other children. But the truth is that, the victor in life is the person who makes the race their own and not what others want him to run.

> *"Many times the victor in life is the person who makes the race their own".*

THE SELF – DISCOVERY PROCESS

The greatest enemy of mankind is ignorance of self. Nothing is more frustrating than not knowing who you are or what has been deposited in you by God and what to do with what you have. Because we lack understanding of who we are and what we are capable of doing, life becomes an experiment, and frustration is the reward.

The greatest discovery in human experience is self-discovery. Self-discovery is a vital part of human development. Your destiny comes alive when you become aware of your true nature - who you truly are. But the problem is that, most people don't understand themselves and that's why they don't yet possess themselves. That is why people who don't know who they are imitate other people and become someone other than who they were created to be.

If you don't know what you were born to be and do, then you become a victim of other people's options. Understanding who made you and who you are is crucial so that others do not take possession of your life. When you have understanding of who you are and what you have, you know what to do with your life.

> *When you have understanding of who you are and what you have, you know what to do with your life.*

The answer to what you excel at lies inside of you, and is reflected in the everyday (as well as the usual) tasks you are already great at, or could be with a little training. This process must start within you. To find them, you need to take a journey inside yourself to discover what they are. Once you become aware of your gifts and talents, your life can begin to change. How?

- Your confidence goes up because you start to realize how gifted and talented you really are.
- You begin to recognize and take advantage of opportunities to excel when you realize "hey I can do that".
- You start to notice the gifts and talents you already use and start thinking about how to take them to the next level of development.
- Overtime, as more ideas keep surfacing, your ideas about who you are and what you can excel at keep evolving.

But the issue is that, few of us really discover, develop and use our gifts and talents. Many die and go to the grave with their God given gifts and talents without discovering and using them. This is the biggest tragedy of life. Instead, we are using the everyday skills we learned in school to earn our living. Our resumes and the jobs they are aimed at are centered on the same set of skills everyone else learned in school. This is why many of us are competing for the same jobs – because we all sell the same skills to our employers. There is nothing unique about what we offer the world. It's dangerous when we try to do the same thing because it causes us to compete instead of complete (compliment) each other.

> *Few of us really develop and use our gifts and talents. Instead, we are using the everyday skills we learned in school to earn our living.*

Look inside yourself, try to identify your strongest gifts and talents, reinforce them with practice and learning, and then find your God-given purpose for your life that draws on these gifts and talents every day. When you do, "you will be more productive, more fulfilled, and more successful." Most people believe that their greatest improvement will come from overcoming their weaknesses. But I believe that, your greatest improvement will come from identifying your natural gifts and talents, developing (strengthening) them and then applying them.

But the truth for some of us is that our gifts and talents mostly go unrecognized, untapped and undeveloped. Yet they are one of the things that make us unique and special on this planet. You are the only person who has your set of gifts and talents.

> *Instead, we are using the everyday skills we learned in school to earn our living.*

The bestselling author, **Brian Tracy** said in his book: **Change Your Thinking Change Your Life** that, "We all have absolutely amazing untapped gifts, talents and abilities that, when properly unleashed and applied, can bring us everything we could ever want in life". Everyone have to spend a little time analyzing himself/herself and rethinking his or her life direction. Each person must begin to ask himself/herself, what is it that he/she really ought to be doing? What are you really good at? Each person must start evaluating his/her gifts and talents - an important step when choosing a career.

THE JOURNEY INSIDE YOU

Everyone has a natural talent or gift. But many of us share a common mistake: we tend to think that what we do, "It's so easy and natural that we tend to under value it, assuming anyone could do what we do so well. But that is wrong. Nobody can do what you are gifted to do. To find your gifts and talents you have to do a self-analysis. It's important to find out the right answers to the following questions if you must discover your gifts and talents. Take the time to reflect on them as you find out the answers to them.

1. **WHAT YOU DO THAT SEEMS ESPECIALLY EASY AND NATURAL.**

   This is an indication of a special talent, or the aptitude for developing such a gift or talent. Notice what people tell you about yourself when you do the things that are easy to do. Do they notice that you light up when you explain something? Does everybody seem to compliment you on your writing, singing, sewing, teaching or something that is easy and you do it so well? What do you seem to be naturally good at? Don't under value it at all. The key to your greatness may lie there.

2. **WHAT YOU DO JUST FOR THE SENSATION OF FULFILLMENT AND SATISFACTION.**

   Consider your interests. What sort of things do you like to read about, write about, or talk about? Is there anything you will do even if there is no money involved but for the sheer satisfaction and fulfillment you get out of it? What shows do you watch on television? What magazine and newspaper articles catch your eye? Etc. These activities are clues to your natural gifts or talents. Your greatest personal potential may lie here.

3. **WHAT YOU DO WHEN TIME JUST SEEMS TO "FLY BY".**

   Such "time distortion" often occurs when we are engaged in an activity we have a passionate and natural love for. Think about what you love to do. What do you usually enjoy doing, without being asked? On what do you focus best or most enthusiastically? What must you be dragged away from doing? Please don't ignore them.

4. **NOTICE WHAT YOU'RE NOT GOOD AT, TOO.**

   What seems always to be a struggle? What makes you feel awkward or out of place? For instance, some people are great talkers but hate writing; for others, it's the other way around. That's not to say you can't develop skills and strategies in areas that are not your forte. It's important to know the things that you do that makes you very uncomfortable and not yourself.

Imagine if you could spend your time just doing something that's easy, makes time fly, and makes you feel happy and fulfilled. Does that sound like a more satisfying life than struggling to become an accountant if you're naturally an artist? Or struggling to become an artist if you're really a natural mechanical engineer or inventor? Why not consider refocusing your life and get the immense satisfaction that comes with being superb at something you love? Even if this requires settling for "less money" or "less prestige" – having a happy, fulfilling life might be an even greater reward. And who knows – your true passion might take you soaring to the top, doing something you truly and naturally love. When a man has found that thing which he will do for free, simply for the fulfillment of doing it, he has found the area of his gifts or talents leading to his calling. Your life is your amazing creation.

Steve Jobs, co-founder, chairman, and CEO of Apple Inc. once said, "You've got to find what you love. And that is as true for your work as it is for your lover. Your work is going to fill a large part of your life, and the only way to be truly satisfied is to do what you believe is great work. And the only way to do great work is to love what you do". If you haven't found it yet, keep looking and don't settle. As with all matters of the heart, you'll know when you find it. So keep looking. Don't settle.

A CASE STUDY:

I will like to use one of my special friends, Miss Afua Aiddo of "AfuAfua" clothing, a fantastic fashion designer, to explain how you can identify your natural gifts and talents. This is a friend I've grown to like so much. We've been friends for the past 18 years and still counting. She initially worked at Association of Rural Banks as a secretary, but at the same time, she had this natural talent to sew, although she had never been to a fashion school.

She would sew for her friend's on weekends at her leisure time. She had this passion and love for sewing right from her youth. For years she treated sewing as a hobby- as something she just loved to do and so gave the bank work her full attention. She stayed at the bank because that was the skill she went to school to learn, and so neglected her natural talent which was sewing. Though she had never been to a fashion school, any time she sewed for her friends they were amazed at her unusual sewing skills. Some of her friends wondered why she was still at the bank and not rather into sewing. She did not initially realize that sewing which was her gift or talent was what needed her full attention. Most people prefer to work a job to earn a salary instead of creating their own products through their gifts and talents.

> *Most people prefer to work a job to earn a salary instead of creating their own products through their gifts and talents.*

As time went on she began to feel uncomfortable with her work at the bank. The desire to develop the sewing career grew and eventually she decided to quit the bank work and go into sewing. Within three years in her sewing business, her products were being patronized by notable people. Her products were unique and her method of marketing them very effective. Because that was her natural talent, the ideas to make it work came to her naturally too.

It's amazing to see her cut materials for sewing. It seems totally instantaneous and effortless. She easily understood things that some of her colleagues who had been in the same field several years back could not understand. The point is that, she is where she is meant to be by purpose based on her gifts and talents and that made the difference in her life. She could have been at the bank and gotten money but would never have been fulfilled.

There were times she complained about how she felt being "used" at the bank. But for the money, I am sure there were times she would have preferred to stay at home. There is one thing to have money and another thing to make a tremendous impact in your area of calling and find the fulfillment that comes along with it.

OUR GIFTS AND TALENTS ARE FROM BIRTH

If our gifts and talents are primarily natural, then they are given to us at birth. This seems to indicate, at least for those of us who have a spiritual outlook, that talents are divine gifts that provide insights into both calling and career direction. Our gifts and talents are always with us from childhood. They are the things we love to do right from childhood. Some from their childhood loved to sing, some loved to cook. Some would love to teach, some would also love to write etc. and yet as we grow and we get involved in many things, things that our parents, our peers and the society at large think are good for us and so we relegate these passions and gifts in us to the background.

We find ourselves pursuing other people's dreams and passions and we gradually let go of those God given passions which are deep seated in us. These passions and desires in us are the keys to excellent future careers.

> "These passions and desires in us are the keys to excellent future careers".

For me it was the ability to sing, far back in my childhood stages in primary school (Radiantway Preparatory School – Sakaman, South Odorkor). I was a member of the school choir. Then later the passion to write, to preach, and to teach and act, in secondary school (Ghana National College – Cape Coast). I used to preach in the bus whenever I travelled to school from Accra to Cape Coast and also when I travelled back home on vacations.

During these times I will collect the addresses of my hearers in the bus and write to encourage them in their walk with God. Those who replied will tell me how my letters were inspirational and such a blessing to them. I guess that was the beginnings of my writings. I was a member and later the music director of a singing and drama group (Burning Fire) while in secondary School. I have come to realize that all your youthful giftings and talents are indication of what you could do in future. Look inwardly and identify all the gifts and talents that have been with you right from childhood.

Let me give you another illustration: My sister-in-law used to be a hair dresser and was barely making it. But this was a woman who knew how to cook so well. Everyone in the family commented on how nice her food tasted. We all saw how well she could cook and we all enjoyed her food. One day, she had a dream that she was serving food to customers and when she told me I encouraged her to start cooking and selling some food by her saloon shop. With time the selling of the food began to overshadow the hair dressing business. As I share with you her story, she is now into big time catering business. Sometimes she gets orders to cook for as many as five hundred to two thousand people. Somebody who was barely managing life as a hair dresser is now making it big as a caterer. She cooks from morning (6:00am) till night (11:00pm). She currently has two food selling joints, where she sells from morning to night.

When you discover the activities you love doing and are great at doing it, you become unique in that area. When there are big functions like engagements, wedding, funerals etc. people call on her services because that is what she loves to do and also great at doing. Don't just do what everyone is doing thinking you will succeed in it. We are all unique in our design or makeup and as such meant to function differently in life. It is when you function according to your design that you will find fulfillment which leads to destiny accomplishment.

This is how the famous brain surgeon, Dr. Ben Carson of Johns Hopkins Hospital-USA, identified his gifts and talent which informed him on his decision to become neurosurgeon. This is what he said, "I thought, I'm really good at things that require eye-hand coordination. I'm a very careful person. I never knock things over and say, Oops'. He said, "I loved to bisect things when I was a kid growing up; if there was a dead animal or a bug around, I knew what was inside" (meaning, he was responsible for bisecting the dead animal). He said he developed a fascination and love for the human brain during all those years studying psychology. It was when he put all this together that he concluded he would make a fabulous brain surgeon. And indeed he has become an excellent Neurosurgeon in the world, in fact one of the best we could think of. The first Neurosurgeon in the world who separated siamese twins without both of the babies dying. He has brought a lot of innovations to the medical profession which has contributed to the advancement in that area.

GIFTS AND TALENTS POINT THE WAY TO MAXIMUM PERFORMANCE

The wisdom of using individual gifts and talents as the key criteria for making career or work choices is not a new idea. You cannot teach talents, you must select them and then use them.

> *You cannot teach talents, you must select them and then use them.*

The Bible says that, **"Having gifts (qualities) that differ according to the grace given us, let us use them"** - **Romans 12:6a.** When people use their natural gifts and talents as well as their spiritual gifts, they are more productive, easier to manage, and experience greater feelings of success. People generally achieve their highest productivity and work satisfaction when they identify and use their unique gifts, and talents. You must therefore give people the freedom to be themselves. The implication is that you do not try to remold people.

You cannot teach talents, you must identify them, select them and then use them. In fact your best friends should be those who bring out the best in you. I hope this book will be your companion as it inspires you to strive to maximize your life by releasing your hidden gifts and talents for the benefit of the world around you and for your personal fulfillment.

> *"When people use their natural gifts and talents, as well as their spiritual gifts, they are more productive, easier to manage, and experience greater feelings of success".*

In his best-selling book: **Job Shift**, Ken Bridges says, "We are finding that the most successful organizations are made up of people doing what they love (like) to do and believe in doing, rather than of people doing what they are "supposed to" do". You see, the most important corporate resources in this twenty-first century will be gifts and talents. You must therefore put yourself ahead by first discovering yours and then find out the best way to develop them. Your greatest performance in life is directly connected to your unique gifts and talents stored in you.

GIFTS AND TALENTS MISMATCH CAUSES PROBLEMS

Now ask yourself if you would be attracted to a work environment where your gifts and talents are likely to be mismatched and then remolded or to the one where they are matched and unleashed. Though the obvious answer will be yes, it does not mean that it is always easy to follow so. You must make sure that your gifts, and talents match the requirements of any assignment you undertake. When we match people to jobs in which their primary work does not exploits their natural gifts and talents, we condemn them to a future somewhere between failure and mediocrity. But when you match your gifts and talents to the task, you get great results and you benefit.

> *You must make sure that your gifts and talents match the requirements of any assignment you undertake.*

When people are using their gifts and talents, it is like swimming downstream. Going with the current, (your natural bent) is efficient and fun. After a long day of work, you may be tired, but you feel good inside because you have been going with the flow and you have traveled quite a distance. You know you have been highly productive; and, just as important, those who are watching are cheering your progress.

On the other hand, when people are mismatched, it is as if they are swimming upstream. Can they do it? Of course they can, but it requires much more energy, is stressful and exhausting and the progress is slow. Moreover, when the sun rises the next day, there is little excitement about getting back in the water. People generally achieve their highest productivity and work satisfaction when they identify and use their unique gifts, and talents.

> *People generally achieve their highest productivity and work satisfaction when they identify, develop and use their unique gifts and talents".*

Yes, joy, satisfaction, and excellence at work are the natural outcomes when you use your God given gifts and talents. For when we set out in youth and choose careers for external reasons—such as the lure of the salary, the prestige of position, or the pressure from parents or peers—we are setting ourselves up for frustration later in life if the work does not equally suit us for internal reasons, namely our giftedness, and calling. 'Success' (as many define it: physical possessions) may then flatter us on the outside as 'significance' (inner satisfaction) eludes us from the inside".

You may have a nice car, a big mansion and money but you may still not be fulfilled in life. You have sacrificed a fulfilled life for a pleasured life. You look good outside but frustrated inside. And frustrated people are difficult to live with. They transfer their frustration to everyone who comes around them. At the end of life, they feel life has no meaning.

> *You have sacrificed a fulfilled life for a pleasured life. You look good outside but frustrated inside".*

Real life does not consist of the abundance of possessions as Jesus Christ said in the Bible (Luke 12: 15) but rather, it's the fulfillment of your life purpose linked to your gifts and talents. If you are going to be effective as well as fulfilled, you must be prepared to spend out of the rich resources of your own unique gifting and talents. There are countless number of individuals who chose to follow a path other than the one dictated by their gifts and talents. There are painful stories of men and women who chased after someone else's dream, who lived the lives their parents wanted, or who sought only the pot of gold at the end of the rainbow.

Equally, I could write about the stories of fulfillment for those who followed their talents and passions, which are usually connected. Those who desire success (outer) and significance (inner) will do well to discover their own life path through the calling of their gifts and talents. Strengths represent a person's best talents, and they are usually the ones we feel compelled to use. When we use them, it feels right, and we know that we are going with the flow.

COURAGE FOR REPOSITIONING

Some of us are aware of our gifts and talents but because we have neglected them for so long and gotten used to the skills we developed whiles in school, it looks like a difficult task going back to them. It is time to stop associating with the crowd put away your fears and step into your divine destiny. Security is about hanging onto what you've got and not letting go, but true success is about taking risks and moving on, striving for new things. There are many today who want to take steps into various vocations which are in line with their gifts and talents, but who experience certain setbacks. They talk to people who give them advice that further puts them under terrible fear.

People will line up to discourage you, but when those who will support you show up, it makes all of the difference in the world. Finding those special people in life is like panning for gold: you may spend years finding nothing more than dirt and rock, but one day you find the golden nugget you've been looking for making the entire journey worthwhile. I pray that this book become one of the companions to encourage you to your greatest heights in life.

Everyone who has had a new experience in life had to break off from the former. If Thomas Edison can take us from candle to light bulb and the Wright Brothers from ground to flight, then clearly your ability to create anything and everything you want through the gifts and talents God has given to you is limited only by your imagination and tenacity. It's the believers and risk takers who've made the world a better place. When a quitter comes up with a really good reason why something won't work, a winner comes up with two reasons why it will.

The twelve's spies who were sent to spy out the land of Canaan in the book of Numbers in the Bible, is a typical example of what am sharing with you. Ten out of the twelve spies gave reasons why the land though a good one could not be possessed by them, but the other two, Caleb and Joshua gave enough reasons why the same land could easily be taken by them regardless of the people who were already occupying it. And the Bible says that,

> *And Caleb stilled the people before Moses, and said, Let us go up at once, and possess it; for we are well able to overcome it. But the men that went up with him said, we are not able to go up against the people; for they are stronger than we -* **Numbers 13:30-31**

If God says the land is theirs and that, they can take it, and then they can take it no matter what. The people with the winner attitude; the, it's possible' mentality will always know that with God all things are possible. Refuse to let anything stop you from entering into your God ordained destiny for you, either through fear or unbelief. Our lives can only become whatever our current beliefs or attitudes allow us to conceive for ourselves.

Like my special friend, Afua Aiddo, (the banker turned fashion designer), people called her all manner of names. People asked her; why she should leave a well-paying job to enter into a business she is not even sure of its future? But at the end of the day she was proved right. Your own determination may be a threat to others if you're attempting something they were and are unable or too afraid to do themselves. You see, when David made up his mind to fight Goliath, his older brothers who were in the army stood against him simply because they could not dare Goliath *(1 Samuel 17: 28-31).*

It is those who are fearful who will oppose you when you want to take a step of faith to carry out what God is creating in your heart. You must always turn away from such people who do not believe in you and turn to those who will listen to you and even create opportunities for you to explore your gifts and talents. You must always draw from past victories and experiences in God to confront present situations. If you can gather the courage to follow the promptings you are receiving in your heart concerning your placement in destiny, which are always connected to your gifts and talents, you will finally be the happiest. You will always need courage if you must fulfill your life calling or dreams. Courage is absolutely indispensable in the accomplishment of your dreams. Yes it takes courage to live life to the full and that courage is yours in Jesus name. Decide to rise, and you will. No matter how deep the pit is, a man of courage soon finds his way out of it, with a smile on his face. You will need to dare your present situation if your future must fall in line with God's purpose for your life.

> *You will always need courage if you must fulfill your life calling or dreams.*

My friend Miss Afua Aidoo, (the fashion designer), told me that, it really took a lot of courage before she could shift from the bank work to start her fashion business. It will always take courage if you must move into your God ordained purpose for your life which has a direct bearing on your gifts and talents. When God called Joshua after the death of Moses to lead the Israelites into the Promised Land, God instructed him to be strong and courageous. This is what the Bible says,

> *"Be strong and of a good courage: for unto this people shall thou divide for an inheritance the land, which I swore unto their fathers to give them. Have not I commanded thee? Be strong and of a good courage; be not afraid, neither be thou dismayed: for the LORD thy God is with thee whithersoever thou go"* - **Joshua 1:6&9**

Many people today feel unfulfilled in their lives, merely going to work at some mundane job, trying to earn a living, stuck in a career they don't even like. When you are not pursuing the dreams and desires God has placed within your heart, you will feel frustration and tension building within you. You feel unhappy about where you are and what you do.

> *"When you are not pursuing the dreams and desires God has placed within your heart, you will feel frustration and tension building within you".*

In using our gifts and talents, we must also make sure that we are using them for the purpose for which they were given to us by God. In the next chapter we will be looking at how to discover God's purpose for your life. We will look at the purpose for which God gave you the gifts and talents that you have. It's important you discover God's purposes for your gifts and talents so you don't abuse them. Dr. Myles Munroe, bestselling author, puts it this way: "When the purpose of a thing (a gift or talent) is not known, abuse is inevitable". Abuse is when you use something (e.g. a gift or talent) for a purpose other than what it was originally intended for by the maker or manufacturer.

If the God intended purposes of your gifts and talents are not known, you will surely abuse them at the end. You must not abuse your gifts and talents; else your whole life will be abuse - a life without meaning.

A STORY TOLD BY BRIAN TRACY

Once upon a time, I had a good friend who was a lawyer in a small firm. His father had been a lawyer so he had taken law when he went to the university. When he got out of school in his early 20s, he began practicing law amongst his friends and associates. But he soon decided that law was not for him. He decided to make a career in business instead. By this time he was about twenty-six years old. In the face of considerable opposition, he gathered all his resources and concentrated single-mindedly on getting into Harvard University to attend its MBA program. It took him two years, but he finally achieved it. It then took him two more years to complete the required courses and graduate with a coveted Harvard MBA.

He returned to his home city and interviewed for various jobs, finally taking an entry – level management position at a rapidly growing airline. It turned out to be a perfect career move. Within ten years he was the president of the airline and earning ten times as much as any of the lawyers that he had graduated with some years before.

He became one of the youngest and most respected executives in charge of a major company in the country. It's your turn and it's not too late.

CHAPTER ONE:
PRINCIPLES

1. Many times the victor is the person who makes the race their own.

2. Yes, joy, satisfaction and excellence at work are the natural outcomes when you lead (unfold and release) gifts and talents - yours and others.

3. You are the only person who has your set of gifts, talents and potentials to excel at the unique task, which define your destiny and your life calling.

4. The key to excellent performance, of course is finding the match between your talents and your role (job).

5. When people are using their natural gifts and talents they are more productive, easier to manage, and experience greater feelings of success.

6. Profitability increases in organizations in which peoples gifts and talents are recognized and developed.

7. The most successful companies are those that value and develop the gifts and talents of their people.

8. Give people freedom to be themselves. You don't try to remold them.

9. The most successful organizations are made up of people doing what they like\love to do and believe in doing, rather than of people doing what they are supposed to do.

10. The most important corporate resource in this twenty-first century will be gifts and talents.

11. Endeavors succeed or fail because of the people involved. Only by attracting the best people will you accomplish great deeds.

12. People generally achieve their highest productivity and work satisfaction when they identify and use their unique gifts and talents.

13. When you are not pursuing the dreams and desires God has placed within your heart, you will feel frustration and tension building within you.

14. You will always need courage if you must fulfill your life calling or dreams.

15. You have sacrificed a fulfilled life for a life of pleasure. You look good outside but frustrated inside".

16 You cannot teach gifts and talents, you must select (find) them and then use them.

17 Instead of finding our gifts and talents and using them, we are using the everyday skills we learned in school to earn our living.

18 Gifts and talents are the keys to organizational and person success.

19 Destiny has gifts and talents.

CHAPTER TWO

GOD'S PURPOSE FOR YOUR GIFTS AND TALENTS

"The greatest secret to finding your God given purpose is to seek God with all of your heart, all of your soul and all of your body."

- Joseph Boateng -

Confusion over personal identity is a global problem. Most of the world is suffering from what I call the "consequences of ignorance of purpose." In every nation, in every community, no matter what language the citizens speak or what colour their skin is, people are experiencing a common dilemma. They are suffering the debilitating effects of a misconception of purpose. They don't understand who they really are, and, therefore, they aren't living up to their full potential in life. In fact, they are destroying their own and others' potential.

The world's crisis of identity is a powerful opportunity for helping others find their true purpose in God.

There is no way that we can have a safe and productive world as long as humanity, as a whole, doesn't know its reason for existence. The world's crisis of identity, therefore, is not just a distressing problem. It is also a powerful opportunity for helping others to find their true purpose in God. Everything God does is motivated by a definite purpose. The original purpose for a product determines its design, composition, capacity, and potential. The principle is that whatever the creator established as the original purpose for his creation determined its natural, its raw material, and its capacity, capability, gifts, natural talents, and potential.

DEFINITION OF PURPOSE:

Purpose is defined as the reason for the existence of something or what someone had in mind for creating a thing. Dr. Myles Munroe says that, purpose is the discovery of a reason for your existence and it is the original intent for the creation of a thing.

PRINCIPLES OF PURPOSE

Dr. Myles Munroe highlighted some principles as they relate to purpose which I will want to outline here to bring clarity to what purpose is about. He said,

- Purpose determines (design)makeup
- Purpose determines potential
- Purpose determines natural abilities
- Purpose determines natural gifts

- Purpose determines natural talents
- Purpose determines fulfillment and personal satisfaction
- Purpose is the source of passion
- Purpose gives existence meaning
- Purpose is the measure of success and failure

THE POWER OF PURPOSE

Purpose is what should drive a person into action whereas importance slows or kills enthusiasm. If you know what God is asking you to do for Him or what your purpose in this life is, then start to pursue it with all of your heart. People rather prefer to do things that make them feel important. Being important or looking important matters to them than fulfilling destiny. They want to do things that are popular with the society (people) because they get their satisfaction from people. They turn to be men pleasers and therefore end up not pleasing God and therefore not having a fulfilled life. It is possible to do good things but not the things that are best based on God's purposes for you. One of the devils greatest weapon against your life is to get you busy doing things that are good but that are not right and best for you.

God created each of us with a purpose. That purpose is what is right for us. Suppose Jesus had become a tax collector or a priest in the Sanhedrin, the highest council and tribunal of the Jews. That would have been a good thing. Suppose he had become a member of the Pharisees and been one of the leaders in the social structure of Galilee and Judea like the Apostle Paul used to be before his conversion. That would have been a good thing. Suppose he had become a social worker, helping the poor, feeding multitudes of people every day with bread and fish. Would that have been a good thing? Sure.

Suppose he had devoted every hour to healing the sick and raising the dead. That would have been a good thing, wouldn't it? Yet none of these things would have been the right thing for Him in fulfilling His chief purpose of being the Saviour of humanity. We must know the purpose for our life and not be distracted with things that are merely good. We must pursue our highest purpose.

It is possible to do good things but not the things that are best based on God's purposes for you.

Purpose is of God whereas importance is of self. If you seek your purpose and pursue it, then you have found God and his blessings, but if not then you are still walking in failure as far as God is concerned. If there is no pursuing of God's purpose in one's life, then there is pursuing of self - of one's own plans and ambitions, which will eventually lead to frustrations and un-fulfillment.

Proverbs 19:21 says that, **"Many are the plans in a man's heart, but it is the purpose of God that will prevail"**. We can fight against His purpose, but if we do, we will be unfulfilled and frustrated. He made us the way we are for His purposes and not for our personal purposes. The number one agenda in any man's life is to find out the purpose of God for his or her life and pursue it passionately.

> *"The number one agenda in any man's life is to find out the purpose of God for his or her life and pursue it passionately".*

There can be no fulfillment and joy in life until one finds out God's purpose for his or her life and pursue it to its fullness. Obedience to God's purpose brings peace and satisfaction in life, but disobedience brings pain, sorrows and eventually emptiness. It is costly to disobey God by not finding out your purpose and fulfilling it. The price you pay for fulfilling your purpose in life is far less than the price you pay for not fulfilling your purpose in life. The purpose of God in one's life is what places value on that person's life. Your gifts and talents give hint of purpose and purpose brings direction and direction brings fulfillment (destination) in life.

> *"The purpose of God in one's life is what places value on that person's life".*

In this life and specifically in the body of Christ, things are not placed in order of importance, but in order of purpose. There is nothing like one thing being more important than the other, but

God has given and distributed every gift and talent according to its purpose. A gift or talent makes no one more important than the other, but rather it gives one a purpose for living. Purpose is therefore more important to God than importance. None of the gifts of God was designed to place importance on any one, but were rather designed to give purpose to one's life. Anyone who feels important because of the gift and talent of God upon his or her life is already living a failed life.

> *"For I say, through the grace given unto me, to every man that is among you, not to think of himself more highly than he ought to think; but to think soberly, according as God has dealt to every man the measure of faith. For as we have many members in one body, and all members have not the same office: So we, being many, are one body in Christ, and every one members one of another. Having then gifts differing according to the grace that is given to us, whether prophecy, let us prophesy according to the proportion of faith; Or ministry, let us wait on our ministering: Or he that teaches, on teaching; Or he that exhorts, on exhortation: he that gives, let him do it with simplicity; he that rules, with diligence; he that shows mercy, with cheerfulness".* - **Romans 12: 3-8**

The human body though united together has several different parts, performing different functions according to their several purposes in the body. They all exist according to their purposes.

One member is not more important than the other. They all have their several purposes to fulfill in the body. The function of the hand is different from that of the leg. The mouth has a different function than that of the ears. No member's contribution to the body is superior to the others and no member can survive by itself. They all need each other if the body must fulfill its overall functions. All the various body parts fulfill its unique purposes in the body. The day a body part feels more important than the other parts, there will be confusion in the whole body.

It is important for us to know that just as the various parts of the human body have their unique purposes to fulfill in the body for its overall function, so does every member of Christ have a specific role to play. No one in the body of Christ is more important than the other, but we all have our unique purposes to fulfill in order to accomplish the overall plans of God for mankind. The scripture above says that, whatever you have been called to do in the body of Christ, you must do it according to the grace of God upon your life. Fulfilling your destiny in life according to the will of God is what matters to God and not how important you feel about yourself.

Whatever you do for God, only defines your purpose in life and not how important you are. The callings of God are not based on how important you are, but according to His purpose for your life. A man, who knows his purpose in life and walks in it, is a very successful man in the sight of God. Every man has the ability to accomplish everything their God - given purpose demands.

The evidence is mounting that the most successful people are those who value and develop their gifts and talents in fulfilling their God given purposes. Life's purpose is discovered, when each individual determines where their passion and gifts meet.

> *Purpose is more important to God than importance.*

YOU WERE CREATED FOR A PURPOSE

Discovering the truth about us is our most important pursuit, and the truth about us is found only in the manufacturer (God). The famous question of history has always been "What is truth?" the most practical definition of truth I have discovered is **"original information."** But the only one who knows the truth (the original information) about anything is the one who created it, for only the originator would have original information about his product.

> *The most practical definition of truth I have discovered is "original information".*

Every person born into this world is sent here to fulfill a certain specific purpose of God. It is a fact that every manufacturer makes a product to fulfill a specific purpose, and every product is designed with the ability to fulfill this purpose. It means that, the potential of a product is determined by its purpose. You cannot just look at a thing and determine what it's capable of doing.

Looks, don't tell what a thing is capable of doing. That's why you cannot look at a person and just determine what that person is capable of doing and becoming. Whether a person is tall or short, fat or slim, white or black, does not give any indication of what the person is capable of doing and becoming. If you want to know what a person is capable of doing and becoming in life, check the divine purpose of God for his/her life. Purpose is what determines the potential of a person. And for your information everything has potential. This is true of everything God created, including you.

Before you were born, your kind of purpose was the reason God endowed you with the kind of gifts and talents that you have. These gifts and talents are meant to uniquely suit your life purpose. Our potentials correspond to our purposes in life. That's why when your purposes in life are not known, your potentials are abused. Because we are creatures of God and he has endowed us with divers kinds of gifts and talents, it will take only God to reveal our individual purposes for the gifts and talent we have. If you want to know your purpose, you can only know it by going to the manufacturer (God) to ask him.

Thus, the purpose of a thing cannot be discovered by asking another thing. It is only the manufacturer of a product who can truthfully show you the reason for creating a product. That's why Christ Himself said, "I have come down from heaven, not to do my own will, but to do the will of him who sent me". Do you know who sent you here on earth? Do you know why He sent you in the first place? You need to find answers to these questions if your life must find meaning. God has given to you, ideas and creativity, as well as specific areas in which you can excel. You are not just here on the earth by the will of your parents, but by God's divine counsel to fulfill a specific purpose. It is imperative that each person finds out God's original purpose for sending him/her to this world. Any life outside of God's will or purpose is a life not properly lived. Your mother and father's desires for you will never be enough to sustain your motivation. Your husband and wife's desire and dream for you will not help you. You must pursue those dreams, and goals, which you really believe are God-inspired, God-intended, and that utilize your gifts, and talents. When you want what you do to have eternal value before God, then you need to find out God's purpose for the gifts, and talents that you have.

Knowing your purpose in life, then allows you to pour all your life experiences, all your gifts and talents, all your wisdom and knowledge into it to impact or make a difference in life. The Bible says that,

> "Many plans are in a man's mind (heart), but it is the Lord's purpose for him that will stand". - **Prov. 19:21**

If what you are pursuing is from God for your life, you will surely succeed, leading to a fulfilled life. Your purpose in life is your ticket or your approval for being alive on this earth. If you fail to achieve your purpose, then you are forfeiting or rejecting the reason for being alive, and this is very dangerous. If you decide not to pursue God's purpose for your life, then you are walking contrary to your makeup or design. The nature of any gift or talent is not based on one's own will or interest but the purpose for which the gifts or talents were given. The possibility of accomplishing one's own goals at the expense of God's purpose for his or her life is so high, if there is no relationship with God. Many have pursued goals and met them, but they have no fulfillment and continually ask why. Accomplishments without a sense of purpose, which comes from God, are meaningless.

> *Your purpose in life is your ticket or your approval for being allowed into this earth. Without it you have no business being here but with it, nobody has any business denying you access.*

Life without an understanding of life's purpose leads to disillusionment and emptiness. Purpose is the reason why something was made. Your purpose is the reason why you were born. It is the key to your fulfillment. Don't be busy amassing wealth, but be busy fulfilling your destiny. Life does not consist of the abundance of possessions, but the emptying of oneself in fulfilling one's purpose in this life. You must die empty by pouring your gifts and talents into your God ordained purposes in life. Don't pour your gifts and talents into the wrong places and purposes. The use of our gifts and talents without their corresponding God's purposes is an abuse and a waste of resources.

> *The possibility of accomplishing one's own goals at the expense of God's purpose for his or her life is so high, if there is no intimate relationship with God.*

I want you to walk away from this book feeling as if you've tapped into a purpose for your life. To a certain degree we all want to know what God has called us to do because there is a certain measure of fulfillment that comes with understanding purpose. When you've really tapped into purpose your life start making sense and we start understanding why we had to go through this or why we had to go through that. Purpose just gives us a reason to go on.

What I want people to understand is that everything that they ever need is locked up inside of them and it's important that we tap into that, otherwise we start moving aimlessly and nobody has time for that. What I want you to know is that, your purpose is not in any man, it's not in any woman; it's not in a job and it is certainly not in a bottle. We just have to discover what that is really, by connecting with our source who is God and then He will show us His plan for our lives. My prayer is that you will find it out, so that you can begin to have a meaningful and purposeful life.

DISCOVER TO RECOVER

The problems of life, arise due to the fact that the purposes for the gifts and talents that people have which is to solve the confusions of life have not yet been discovered. The delay to discover is the delay to be fulfilled.

The delay to discover is the delay to be fulfilled.

Man is not called by God to create anything new, but he is called to just discover what has already been created by God. We are not supposed to create our own purposes in life, but we are to discover them. One of two pioneers of the motivational speaking industry in Ghana, Emmanuel Dei-Tumi once said and I quote, "Your purpose is not yours to decide, it is yours to discover."

The multitude of problems or needs of man is an indication that there are more discoveries to be made in the area of our purpose in life. Until we know our God given purposes in life, many of the problems people are facing will not be solved. Each person's purpose is meant to solve a specific problem of man. The more discoveries of the purposes of man that is made, the fewer problems we will have. The answers to our problems are not to be created by us; they are rather to be discovered by us with the help of the Holy Spirit. Until you understand that you are rather to discover your purposes in life, you will waste time and energy trying to create a different purpose for your life which at the end will create frustrations, leading to dissatisfaction in your life. To discover your God given purpose in life is easier; it requires a search of what God has already planned for you before you were born.

Remember that, God creates, man discovers and a reverse of this principle creates difficulties and in fact it is the reason for all of man's difficulties. Discoveries of life purposes produce the keys that open the doors to solutions to problems in people's lives. What man is looking for is not in what he is creating, but it is in what God has already created. That is why after all that man does he is still not satisfied with himself. The more discoveries you make concerning your life destiny, the more recoveries you will have. The degree of discovery you make concerning your God given purpose in life, will determine the degree of revolution you cause on this earth.

> *God creates but man discovers and the more discoveries you make concerning your life purpose, the more recoveries you will have.*

When God talks of harvest, he's talking about bringing increment, enlargement and fruitfulness to what he has placed in your heart that you are pursuing. Until you are planting what he has placed in your heart (purpose), you will not experience the harvest he has promised you. Whatever a man sows that is what he will reap. Otherwise you will be receiving the trickles of other people's harvest. Your future success is not ahead of you but right on the inside of you. You are a treasure to be discovered, dug and released for the benefit of mankind. Remember that this treasure is buried in the earthen vessel of your body (2 Corinthians 4:7).

Be committed to your purpose in life without wavering and the God of harvest will cause it to increase. Listen, you will not harvest if you invest in any other work apart from where you are supposed to be according to God's purpose for your life. It is doing what you are called to do by God that guarantees harvest. Your harvest is connected to the seed in you. Harvest always springs from seeds. Anytime your purpose in life is being attended to, you are just stirring up your harvest for manifestation. When your harvest time comes the hand of God will be your help as you pursue your purpose in this life. Don't compare yourself with anyone else, you may be tempted to do as other people are doing. God's plan for you is different, and the way to everyone's harvest is not the same. Concentrate on your path towards your harvest. Someone's path to his harvest might be the path to your famine and shame.

There are specific instructions to specific individuals on how to enter their harvest in life when the right time comes. God will surely guide and lead you in the way that you should go into profiting.

Your purpose is not yours to decide, it is yours to discover.

YOUR PURPOSE IN LIFE THROUGH CHRIST JESUS

The natural man (i.e. the person who is not born again) is confused when it comes to the whole issue of God because his senses – the sense of touch, smell, sight, taste and hearing cannot connect him to the supernatural God and therefore does not know or understand God. The Bible says that, "The natural man receives not the things of the Spirit of God: for they are foolishness unto him; and he cannot know them, because they are spiritually understood" - *1 Corinthians 2:14*

> *"Because the mind of the flesh (senses) is enmity against God, for it is not subject to the law of God, neither indeed can it be; and they that are in the flesh (senses) cannot please God."* - **Romans 8:7** *(The emphasis are my own)*

By the five senses the natural man has been able to study and understood the material world, even to the point of travelling to the moon, but the natural man has not yet known the supernatural God, because God cannot be fully understood only through our senses. God is a spirit although he created the physical world we live in. We as human beings are also spirit beings though we live in physical bodies.

Any person who is not born again (natural man) is spiritually dead and cannot connect to the supernatural God. His spirit is dead, and until it's recreated by the Spirit of God, he cannot receive and know the things which are of God. It is when a person is born again and then filled with the Spirit of God, that such a person can enjoy a walk with God. The supernatural life is not possible without the operation of the Holy Spirit (the Spirit of discovery and truth). In fact without the Holy Spirit, man will be cut off from knowing the supernatural God and also knowing what the supernatural God has in store for him. The Holy Spirit is the revealer of the mysteries of the divine purposes of God concerning your life.

God gave us bodies which have the five senses so that we can contact the physical world. But to contact God, He recreated our spirits through salvation by the power of the Holy Spirit called the born again experience. He then filled us with His Holy Spirit, so we can stay in contact and be able to communicate with Him. The only way to have a personal relationship with God which leads to a discovery of one's life purpose is through his son Jesus Christ. Those who receive Jesus as their Lord and savior (born again) have the opportunity to be filled with the Holy Spirit. The Holy Spirit then becomes the revealer of the mysteries of God for your life. The Bible says that,

> "Jesus is the way, the truth and the light, no one goes to the father except through Christ Jesus" - **John 14:6.**

It is only when you acknowledge Jesus Christ as your Lord and savior; that you can be recreated. For all have sinned and fallen short of the glory of God. It's when you believe in your heart, that he died and rose for the forgiveness of your sins and confesses with your mouth of his lordship over your life, that you are restored back to fellowship with God. If you don't believe in the master then it will be difficult for you to understand the master plan. The truth is that you must be born again.

THE NICODEMUS ENCOUNTER WITH JESUS CHRIST

> *"Now there was a man of the Pharisees, named Nicodemus, a ruler of the Jews; this man came to Jesus by night and said to Him, "Rabbi, we know that you have come from God as a teacher; for no one can do these signs that you do unless God is with him." Jesus answered and said to him, "Truly, truly I say to you, unless one is born again he cannot see the kingdom of God." Nicodemus said to Him, "How can a man be born when he is old? He cannot enter a second time into his mother's womb and be born, can he?" Jesus answered, "Truly, truly, I say to you, unless one is born of water and the Spirit he cannot enter into the kingdom of God. "That which is born of the flesh is flesh, and that which is born of the Spirit is spirit. "Do not be amazed that I said to you, 'You must be born again'."*
>
> **- John 3:1-7**

When Nicodemus sought out Jesus by night to question Him privately, he was not really looking for a person; he was looking for a kingdom. He had recognised the power of God at work in the life and activities of Jesus, and it stirred his curiosity. He realised that Jesus had tapped into a dimension of spiritual reality that he had never experienced.

The more Nicodemus saw Jesus manifesting the power and glory of God out of His life, the more he saw that he himself was not living at the full capacity of his life. The more he saw Jesus Christ, the more he realised that there was more to life than what he was doing as a teacher of the law of the nation of Israel. The life and ministry of Jesus gave him more insight about life than what he and his colleague's teachers of the law were doing. Jesus said and did things which were beyond the level at which they were operating. Nicodemus confessed to Jesus, that they knew He had come from God and that God was the one using him. What he didn't understand was why His ministry was gloriously different from theirs as Pharisees. Even though he was a teacher of the law, which was one of the highest ranks in Judaism (the religion of the Jews), he felt he was living far below what God could do through and for him. He therefore secretly came to Jesus by night to discover the secret of the manifestation of the glory and power of God through His life and ministry. Whether by day or by night he was determined to meet Jesus Christ and find out why He was different from them in the way he ministered to the people and the results that accompanied his work. He didn't allow jealousy and envy to rob him of going to find out the secret of this young Hebrew man who was turning the towns and cities of Israel around.

Jesus who saw his desire to know the secret behind all that He did and not to argue with Him concerning what he said and did, told him the secret of the kingdom which makes all kingdom citizens extraordinary. Jesus didn't talk about his natural family background or his educational background, but rather spoke about his spiritual background. He went straight to the point and said, "You must be born again". Born again? Yes born again! This statement threw this teacher of the law into confusion. He wondered how on earth he at his age and stature could be born again. How can he enter the womb of his mother the second time to be born again. While he was looking at the physical side of birth, Jesus was looking at a spiritual birth. Many people are still confused about this born again experience.

Many argue about it and think that it is stupidity. Yes the wisdom of God is always stupid to the natural mind and that's why our natural mind cannot comprehend the supernatural God. It will take a supernatural encounter with the supernatural God to understand the mysteries of the kingdom of God. And so Jesus told Nicodemus, "Assuredly, unless one is born again, he cannot see the kingdom of God". Jesus in effect was saying to this man, it doesn't matter who you are and where you come from, you cannot experience what is in this kingdom except you are born into the kingdom by the word and Spirit of God. Jesus said, "That which is born of the flesh is flesh."

He was saying to him, you were born into this physical world by your parents, but to be part of the kingdom of God and be a partaker of what is in the kingdom, you must be born again by the Spirit of God who gives spiritual birth to new born spiritual babies in the kingdom. Without this spiritual birth experience, you will remain in the realm of the flesh which cannot receive from God. Therefore Jesus said, "That which is born of the Spirit is spirit." This man didn't know how on earth this could be done. Of course we all don't know and understand how we were born physically until we were told how. In the same way we might not understand how this new spiritual birth takes place, but if we can believe the maker of it, we will have a supernatural experience of it that will usher us into a new dimension of a spiritual walk with the King of the kingdom. This is what definitely changes the course of our lives for good.

You can never know the fullness of what God has for your life until you are born into His kingdom and the governor of the kingdom, the Holy Spirit will then begin to coach you and reveal to you the deep things of God concerning your glorious destiny. You can be anything in this natural world like say a doctor, a lawyer, a footballer, businessman, a professor etc. but until you are born again and discover God's original intent for your life, you will not be able to serve Him in the full capacity of your life. Ignorance of who you are and what you can do will deny you the opportunity of having a fulfilled life.

The born again experience is the first step leading to a discovery of God and your God given purpose in this life which leads to a fulfilling life here on earth. Nicodemus was a doctor of the law but something was still missing out of his life until he met Jesus. Can it be that you are not satisfied with yourself because you have not had the born again experience? Jesus might be telling you what He told Nicodemus, "You must be born again - born of the Word and Spirit of God. Only then can you begin to experience what the King of the kingdom has prepared for your destiny. Physically, we are children of men, but spiritually also, we need to be children of God. Until you are born again, you cannot relate to God as your father. You can only relate to Him as God and there is big difference between He being a God and He being a father. Nicodemus related to Him as God, but Jesus related to Him as father. The two types of relationships give different access to the throne room of grace, where we find grace to help us in time of need.

When God is your father you have free access to the throne room of God. He said, "Come boldly to the throne room of grace that you may find grace and mercy to help you in time of need" (Hebrew 4:16). It's only the children of God who have that kind of access to the throne of God. The Israelites couldn't go to the Holy of Holies (throne of grace and mercy). Only the high priest could do that.

The throne of grace is where judgements are averted. As long as the high priest, gets into the holy of holies and performs all the necessary sacrifices, any pending judgement against the Israelites is appeased. As the blood of bulls and goats atoned for the sins of the Israelites, so did the blood of Jesus atones for the sins of the whole world. Yes He is the God of all flesh, but the father of those who are born again.

If you don't have the same Spirit of His son in your heart which makes you cry "Abba father", then you are none of His (Galatians 4:6). The Spirit of adoption that makes you cry "Abba father" is the seed of Gods spiritual DNA in you that qualifies you as His child (Romans 8:15). Can you call God your father and His Spirit also bearing witness with your spirit that indeed you are a child of God? (Romans 8:16). The Bible says that, "The Lord knows those who are His" (2 Timothy 2:19).

You might say that you know Him, but the question is, does He know you? Until you are born again by the Spirit of God, you have no relationship with him. Yes He is a gracious and a generous God who allows rain to fall on the wicked and the righteous as well, but there is a level of intimacy that can only be experienced with Him when we are born again.

Your relationship with God is the foundation upon which you are able to fellowship with God. Having a personal relationship with God then leads you to know the secret information concerning your life as far as God's plans and purposes for your life are concerned.

> *Your relationship with God is the foundation upon which, God can fellowship with you and share the secrets concerning His purposes for your life.*

Saul, who later became Paul the apostle in the New Testament of the Bible, was a zealous Jew and a Pharisee who intensely persecuted the early Christians - the Church, and tried to destroy it. But God had other plans for his life, of which he did not know.

God had a purpose for him far different from what he was doing as a Pharisee because of his family tradition.

He was a Pharisee because his father was a Pharisee. He was busy doing things that were good for a Pharisee but that are not right and best for him according to God's purpose for his life. We will use Paul as a case study of one who encountered God (got born again) and how it led to the discovery of his God given purpose for his life and how it changed the course of his life.

PAUL AS A CASE STUDY:

His Background

Paul was born near the beginning of the first century in the busy Greco-Roman city of Tarsus, located at the Mediterranean Sea. This was a famed trading center noted for the manufacturing of goat's hair cloth, and here the young Saul, (the Hebrew) or Paul (the Greek) version, learned his trade of tent making. By vocation he was a tentmaker. The Bible says, **"And because he was a tentmaker as they were (Priscilla and Aquila), he stayed and worked with them"- Act 18:3**

He was born of purest Jewish blood (Phil. 3:5), the son of a Pharisee (Acts 23:6), and Saul was cradled in Orthodox Judaism. At the proper age, perhaps thirteen, he was sent to Jerusalem and completed his studies under the famous Gamaliel (Acts 22:3; 26:4-5). Being a superior, zealous student (Gal. 1:14), he absorbed not only the teachings of the Old Testament but also the rabbinical learning of the scholars. He was more exceedingly passionate for the traditions of his fathers. He was more zealous than many of his contemporaries. He had a genuine desire or passion for the things of God though it was not according to knowledge or revelation of God. His first appearance in Acts as "a young man" (Acts 7:58), probably at least thirty years old, he was already an acknowledged leader in Judaism. His active opposition to Christianity marked him as the natural leader of the persecution that arose after the death of Stephen (Acts 7:58-8:3; 9:1-2). The persecutions described in Acts 26:10-11 indicate his fanatical devotion to Judaism. He was convinced that Christians were heretics (teaching of false doctrines) and that the honor of the Lord demanded their extermination (Acts 26:9). He acted in confirmed unbelief and ignorance (1 Tim. 1:13).

He was very zealous but not according to the knowledge of God's purpose for his life. Though a tentmaker, he naturally had a zeal for the religion or traditions of his fathers. He was zealous or passionate, thinking he was serving God and preserving the traditions of his father's from the influx of a false religion (Christianity). Yet due to his ignorance of the will and purpose of God for his life, he was going against the very God he claimed to be serving. He had a natural love and zeal (passion) for the things of God, but the purpose of his zeal was wrong.

Paul did not know that God had a different plan and purpose for his life. That passion he had on the inside of him was meant to preach or witness about Jesus Christ and not to persecute Him. He didn't know that the reason for his strong passion for God was to witness about the resurrected Jesus Christ and not to persecute Him. Your natural passions must be accompanied with revelation or knowledge of the will and purpose of God for that in born passion.

Zeal without knowledge is a disaster; for lack of knowledge of the agenda of God for your life is what leads to vanity at the end of life. God said to Jeremiah,

> "Before you were born, I knew you and ordained you to be a Prophet". - **Jeremiah 1:5**

God had determined to reveal Christ Jesus to Saul so that he might preach Him among the gentiles (Galatians 1:16). He said it pleased God to separate him in his mother's womb that He may reveal the resurrected Christ to him that he might preach about Him to the gentiles. His gifts and talents were for this purpose which he now was fighting against due to his ignorance of the will of God for his life. He had zeal (passion) but it wasn't according to the knowledge of the purpose of God for his life.

His Conversion

The persecution was doubtless opposed to his finer inner sensitivities, but Saul did not doubt the rightness of his course. The spread of Christians to foreign cities only increased his fury against them, causing him to extend the scope of his activities. The

Bible says that as he approached Damascus, one of the cities the persecuted Christians had run to, armed with authority from the high priest, the transformational crisis that brought a change in his life occurred. His conversion can only be explained as a divine intervention. Indeed this was the work of divine grace and power transforming him and later commissioning him as a messenger of Christ. On his way to persecute the Christians who had run to Damascus, Jesus Christ arrested him and revealed himself to him. The Bible says that,

> *"And as he journeyed, he came near Damascus: and suddenly there shined round about him a light from heaven: And he fell to the earth, and heard a voice saying unto him, Saul, Saul, why persecutes thou me? And he said, who art thou, Lord? And the Lord said I am Jesus whom thou persecute: it is hard for thee to kick against the pricks. And he trembling and astonished said, lord, what will thou have me to do? And the Lord said unto him, Arise, and go into the city, and it shall be told thee what thou must do".* - **Acts 9: 3-6**

On the road to Damascus to arrest the Christians there, Saul had a face-to-face encounter with Jesus Christ. It was after Saul had that encounter with Jesus Christ that the course of his life was changed. His life was given a meaningful reason for the zeal (passion) he had in him. By the time Saul got to the city of Damascus, God had revealed to one of the Jewish Christians, named Ananias the purpose of God for Saul's life. It was after Paul had met the Lord or better still, it was after the Lord had arrested him that God's purpose for his life was revealed to him. That encounter changed Saul's life forever. Saul the Pharisee became Paul the Apostle. If he had not met Christ, he would have been a Pharisee all his life and not fulfilled his life purpose as an apostle to the Gentiles. You are not here on earth to carry out your personal agenda or the agenda of men, but to fulfil a God given assignment.

Those things that you are passionate about are indications of what to pursue with your life but you need a clear defined purpose from God as to how to do it. God gave him the right purpose for his inborn passions. This is what the Lord said about Saul to Ananias,

> *"But the Lord said unto him (Ananias), go thy way: for he (Saul) is a chosen vessel unto me, to bear my name before the Gentiles and kings and the children of Israel; for I will show him how great things he must suffer (fulfil) for my name's sake".* - **Acts 9:15-16**

From Paul's own mouth he told of the purpose for which Jesus Christ arrested him on the road to Damascus. He told King Agrippa why Jesus Christ had called him,

> *"I am sending you to them to open their eyes and to turn them from darkness to light, and from the power of Satan to God, so that they may receive forgiveness of sins and a place among those who are sanctified by faith in me".*
> - **Acts 26: 18**

God had set Saul apart before his birth for this very purpose. His purpose in life or purpose for being called was clearly defined. His purpose was clearly spelt out. **What** he was to do, **how** he was to do it and the **end results** after he has done it were all spelt out for him. Even his audience (the gentiles) was defined for him. Every purpose of God for any man has a certain group of people it's meant to affect.

Your purpose in life must have these key elements; **the what (vision), the how (mission) and the end results (outcome)**. This will make it easier to measure your progress in the assignment God has called you to do for him. The Bible says that,

> *"But when it pleased God, who separated me from my mother's womb and called me through His grace, to reveal His son (Jesus Christ) in me, (Saul) that I might preach Him among the gentiles, I did not immediately confer with flesh and blood".* - **Galatians 1:15-16.**

It was right from his mother's womb that God ordained and set him apart to reveal His son Jesus Christ to him, so he might preach Him among the gentiles. This was God's purpose for his life and at the right time He called him through His grace. This purpose was from birth and was revealed to him at the appointed time.

DETAILS OF SAUL'S PURPOSE:

The What: Paul's Vision

- To open the eyes (of understanding) of people (the Gentiles) to the gospel of grace of the Lord Jesus Christ.
- To turn them from spiritual darkness to light, which is in Jesus Christ.
- To deliver them from the power of Satan to God. (Acts 26: 1-15)

The How: Paul's Mission

- By the preaching of the gospel of Jesus Christ through the power of the Holy Spirit. (For he said, "I am not ashamed of the Gospel of Jesus Christ for it is the power of God unto salvation to the Jews and the gentiles: Romans 1:16, Galatians 1: 11-16).

The End Results:

- That people will receive the forgiveness of sins from God
- That people will then obtain a place (their inheritance) among those who are sanctified by faith in Christ.

He was to preach Christ among the Gentiles, a means to open their eyes of understanding and turn them from darkness to light and from the power of Satan to God. The end result of his purpose was that the Gentiles may come to receive the forgiveness of sins and also to obtain a place among those who are sanctified by faith in Christ.

Every purpose of God must have a desired end result by which you can use to measure if you are doing well or whether you are on track or not. That's why Paul could confidently say, "I have fought a good fight, I have finished my course (my purpose) and I have kept the faith (2 Timothy 4:7). The clearer you are about what you want and what you have to do to achieve it, the easier it is for you to overcome procrastination and get on with the completion of the task. What is your purpose in life? It's time to discover God's purpose for your life, so you can start to live a purposeful, meaningful and fulfilled life. Uncertainty must come to an end in your life as you begin a new life of purposeful living through Christ Jesus.

Saul's purpose in life was not to become a Pharisee, persecute the Christians and be a fanatic, but it was rather to make Christ well known to people (especially the Gentiles) and strengthen the Christians. Can you imagine that before he met Christ, he was rather doing the opposite of his life purpose? He had the zeal or passion, but because he lacked revelation or insight of that specific assignment, he rather abused his zeal. We have a lot of people who are using their gifts and talents to do things which are opposite of what God has ordained for their lives.

The purpose of God for your life can only be told you by God and this can happen when you come into a personal relationship with God through Jesus Christ. Without a personal encounter with Christ Jesus, you cannot know the real purpose for your existence

– I mean the original purpose of God for the gifts and talents you have. The purposes of God for your life are the reason for your creation. In the book of Jeremiah, God told Jeremiah,

> *"Before I formed thee in the belly I knew thee; and before thou came forth out of the womb I sanctified (set thee apart) thee, and I ordained thee a prophet unto the nations".* **- Jeremiah 1:4-5**

There was a reason for the creation of Jeremiah. Before his conception in the womb, God had a purpose and based on that purpose God initiated his formation in the womb so he can be born to the earth to fulfill that purpose. Based on his purpose, God endowed him with the kind of gifts and talents and personality which are meant to help him achieve that purpose. There is a purpose for every individual created by God which we need to discover in order to create the kind of change we all desire in our lives.

There are many who know their gifts and talents (passions) but because they don't know the purposes for these gifts and talents, are using them to satisfy their own personal interest (ambitions) and what others want them to do. Paul could have continued to use his gifts and talents to destroy the Christians and not know that he was abusing the gifts and talents which God had given to him. There are many who are using their gifts and talents to destroy the very lives for which they've been called to bless, simply because of the purpose they are using them for. Can you imagine someone who has the gift of singing, using this gift to write and sing songs which has the power to corrupt the minds of his hearers? This same gift could have been used to inspire and educate people leading them to achieve their greatest dreams in life.

Knowing your gifts and talents, without knowing the purposes for which God gave them to you is a disaster. We shall all answer to God one day, whether or not we were able to fulfill our life purposes with the gifts and talents we have. It is not enough to discover those gifts and talents and use them, but whether the purpose for which they were given, is the focus of accomplishment.

QUALITY FELLOWSHIP WITH THE HOLY SPIRIT

Every human being is born with gifts and talents from God, but in order for these gifts and talents to reach their maximum potential in service for the Kingdom, they need to be reconnected to their original source. No one really knows the true essence of his gifts and talents unless he reconnects with the Spirit of the creator. Moreover, the Holy Spirit activates our gifts and talents to a level that we wouldn't naturally bring them.

Man was created to function attached to God; he could fulfill his full potential and maximize his full capacity only through his connection with God. The key to effective and successful living is the indwelling Spirit of God-called the Holy Spirit. The Holy Spirit, therefore, is the key to your encounter with your true purpose in life. The Holy Spirit is the critical component in man, because he is the only hope for rediscovering our true identity, self-image, self-worth, significance, self-esteem and destiny (purpose). The Scripture says that,

> *"What eye has not seen and ear has not heard and has not entered into the heart of man, [all that] God has prepared (made and keeps ready) for those who love Him [who hold Him in affectionate reverence, promptly obeying Him and gratefully recognizing the benefits He has bestowed]. [Isa 64:4; 65:17.] Yet to us God has unveiled and revealed them by and through His Spirit, for the [Holy] Spirit searches diligently, exploring and examining everything, even sounding the profound and bottomless things of God [the divine counsels and things hidden and beyond man's scrutiny]. For what person perceives (knows and understands) what passes through a man's thoughts except the man's own spirit within him? Just so no one discerns (comes to know and comprehend) the thoughts of God except the Spirit of God. Now we have not received the spirit [that belongs to] the world, but the [Holy] Spirit who is from God, [given to us] that we might realize and comprehend and appreciate the gifts [of divine favor and blessing so freely and lavishly] bestowed on us by God. And we are setting these truths forth in words not taught by human wisdom but taught by the [Holy] Spirit, combining and interpreting spiritual truths with spiritual language [to those who possess the Holy Spirit]. But the natural,*

non spiritual man does not accept or welcome or admit into his heart the gifts and teachings and revelations of the Spirit of God, for they are folly (meaningless nonsense) to him; and he is incapable of knowing them [of progressively recognizing, understanding, and becoming better acquainted with them] because they are spiritually discerned and estimated and appreciated".
1 Corinthians 2: 9-14 (AMP)

The Holy Spirit reconnects you to the source of your gifts and talents so that you can understand what you have been given – not just the value of your gifts and talents, but also the magnitude of them. This means that no one's intellect alone can discern or understand the gifts and talents that God has placed within him for the purposes of the kingdom. This is why, if you want to know what the Spirit of God really created inside you, you have to connect to the Holy Spirit.

The answer to making outstanding discoveries in life as far as your God's given purpose is concerned lies in the quality of fellowship you have with the Holy Spirit as a child of God. The Holy Spirit is called the Spirit of truth (the Spirit who has the "original information") and therefore without him, no discoveries in the kingdom of God can be made. Your high places in life are directly connected to the discovery of your God's given purpose and the understanding you make in that area of calling (purpose). Remember that the high places of people differ and that, it is the discoveries you make in your area of calling or purpose that will determine your placement in life. Don't joke with discoveries (revelations), for it's your passport to greatness and change. The discovery or revelation of your purpose in this life, will turn out to be the beginning of a great adventure in your life.

> *The answer to making outstanding discoveries in life as far as your God given purpose is concerned lies in the quality of fellowship you have with the Holy Spirit – seek Him with all that is in you.*

The Bible is the source from which all discoveries are made and until you have a question needing an answer, it does not open up to you. The answers in the Bible only respond to questions and the person who has the questions of life and is also full of the Holy Spirit will enjoy the mysteries in the kingdom of God. Until the full purpose of the creation of a gift or talent is discovered, its full benefit and results will not be experienced. It does not matter how you sincerely use a gift or talent, its full blessing will not be release until its divine purpose is the focal point of achievement. Seeking God with all your heart, all of your soul and all of your strength is the secret to finding all of God's purpose for your life. When we seek the manufacture, we will finally find the mind of the maker concerning his purposes for our lives. Lack of our pursuit of God is the reason for many not knowing the God given purpose for their lives.

Many are more concerned with what God can give them in the form of physical blessings and not God's purpose for their lives. The Bible says that, "if we will seek God with all of our hearts, with all of our soul and all of our strength, we will find him and then find ourselves (who we really are) and what we were called to do in this life" (Deut. 6:5). If people will really seek God, they will find themselves at the end and finding ourselves is the beginning of fulfillment in life.

The Discoveries you make in your area of calling that will determine your placement in life.

EVERY GIFT AND TALENT HAS ITS GOD GIVEN PURPOSE

Every gift and talent has a specific purpose to accomplish in this life; if you fail to see the purpose of a gift or talent, then the gift or talent will not be a blessing to people. The power of any gift or talent is its purpose. If you destroy the God intended purpose of a gift or talent, then the gift or talent is of no use to you and the people around you according to the will of God. Then you have abused the gift and talent.

When the purpose of a thing is not known, abuse is inevitable. If the purpose of a gift is not pursued, then there is futility. There can be no achievement apart from the very purpose for which God intended the gift or talent to perform. If you do not achieve the purpose of that gift, you have failed; it is not what you think or what your purpose is, but rather the purpose for which God gave that gift. It is not for fun, it is supposed to accomplish a definite task.

> *Anytime a gift or talent is been used, its God given purpose must be the focal point of achievement.*

DON'T GAIN THE WORLD AND LOSE YOUR SOUL

When you are off your path, your soul will ache. It is not like a toothache, a backache, or a stomach-ache. You feel this pain in the deepest part of your being. There is no medication that will correct it. The only thing that will ease an aching soul is repentance. That word simply means to turn around and go the other way dictated by your God given purpose.

Like all pain, a soul ache is a warning that something is wrong. The pain is an alarm that buzzes and screams when you have chosen a path that alters your course. It indicates that you have stepped out of your destiny and are lost. You see, some things that we try to do just don't fit the course of a God-given purpose. Then the soul aches like your feet in shoes that looked good on you, on the outside, but just don't fit on you, on the inside. You have to know when something doesn't fit. Soul aches can be your compass.

In my city, and likely in yours, there are several ways to get to the same place. I can take any one that I want and still get there. So it is with life. There are many ways that you can go to get to the same place. The path you take is your own choice. What you don't want to do is choose a path that takes you off course. But when you do make a choice that doesn't fit your life plan, God will let you know. Your soul will start to ache. It means that you are on the wrong road to get to the right end. When that happens, you have to say to whom or whatever it is that is making your soul ache, "No, this doesn't work for me. This shoe is not cut for my foot.

The sad thing is that, many people never realize that, soul ache is a sign that they are off their destiny path. They sadly continue that way the rest of their lives and miss the opportunity to have become something remarkable. *"Why art thou cast down, O my soul? And why art thou disquieted within me?"* - **Psalm 42: 11 KJV**

It is wise to occasionally take the time to reflect on where you are and to assess where you are going. But most of all, ask yourself how you are doing. You are probably the only person who will know how you are feeling and really stick around to hear the answer. So many have lost their passion and are living with a disturbed soul, which causes much internal pain. For many, it's a condition that causes restlessness, discontentment, and irritability.

If you have lost your way, pull over to the side of the road and ask for directions. God has the power to provide arrows pointing us back to our proper route. As the Psalmist tells us, "He restores my soul…" (**Psalm 23:3**). If you are not sure that your decisions are lining up with your destiny, and then listen within to the voice of God. He will speak in your soul, and He will restore it.

> "But when Jesus turned and looked at his disciples, he rebuked Peter. "Get behind me, Satan!" He said, "You do not have in mind the things of God, but the things of men." Then he called the crowd to him along with his disciples and said: If anyone would come after me, he must deny himself and take up his cross and follow me. For whoever wants to save his life will lose it, but whoever loses his life for me and for the gospel will save it. What good is it for a man to gain the whole world, yet lose his soul? Or what can a man give in exchange for his soul?" - **Mark 8:33-37**

You lose your soul (soul aches) when you do not have in mind the things of God, but rather the things of men. You are more concerned about the pleasures of this life than the purpose of God for your destiny. Peter was more concerned about his personal interest rather than the purpose of God for him. If you are not careful, people can allow their personal interest to hinder the purpose of God for your life. Anytime we forfeit the purpose of God for our destiny, we lose our soul and allow it to drift off the path of fulfilment. Our soul begins to wonder aimlessly in this world, out of touch with the divine reality of its purpose. The soul then is lost chasing after the amusement of this world instead of the fulfilment of heaven.

Satan wanted to exchange the soul of Christ for the things of this world. He wanted Christ to short change His destiny for the gain of the whole world. The Bible says,

> *"Again, the devil took him to a very high mountain and showed him all the kingdoms of the world and their splendor. "All this I will give you," he said, "If you will bow down and worship me." Jesus said to him, "Away from me, Satan! For it is written: Worship the Lord your God, and serve him only." -* **Matthew 4: 8-10**

The devil takes Jesus to a high mountain where in view he could show Christ the world and the splendor in it and makes a bargain with him in exchange for His destiny purpose on earth. You cannot worship to masters. Whoever you submit to becomes your master and his will you will do. If Jesus submit to Satan and worship him, then it means He has abandoned the purpose of God for the will of Satan. Anytime you abandon the will of God for the splendor of the things of this world, you have lost your soul in exchange.

The Bible says that, "If the love of the world is in you, then the love of the father is not in you. It takes those who love the father, to be committed to the will of the father. Jesus said, "If you love me, you will keep my commandment."

> *Whoever you submit to, becomes your master and his will you will do.*

Proof of your love for the father is seen in your total commitment to the will of the father for your life on earth. If your love for the things of this world is more than your love for the things of His kingdom, then you have given your soul in exchange for things. Your soul is to serve the kingdom of God, whiles the things of this world are to serve you. You were created to do the will of God and the things of this world were created to serve you to do that. That's why Mathew 6:33 says that, "Seek first the kingdom of God and its righteousness and all other things will be added unto you."

Don't chase the things of this world and end up losing your soul along the way. Satan is after your soul and will give you anything in this world in exchange for it. He wants your soul to worship him so that you are forever his, so you miss the plan of God for your life. Remember that the final destination of Satan is hell fire and if you chose to sell your soul to him in exchange for the splendor of this world, and then know where your final end will be too.

Jesus said to him, "Away from me, Satan! For it is written: Worship the Lord your God, and serve him only." I repeat, you were created to worship the Lord your God, and serve him only. Are you committed to worshiping and serving the Lord your God only? Is His will and purpose for your life your utmost concern? Are you ready to lay down your life for His purpose for your life on earth no matter what the cost maybe? Don't allow Satan to make you try to gain the whole world and lose your soul. Remember we will leave all the things of this world here, but God's purpose for our lives will follow us into eternity. He will ask you for what purpose you used the gifts and talents that you had. Return to God in worship and determine to serve His purpose for your life only.

In the next chapter we will be looking at how to develop the gifts and talents you have in order for them to achieve their God given purposes more efficiently and effectively. For example when you are given a cutlass and its purpose is for cutting down trees, the next reasonable thing you do is to find out how the cutlass can be sharpened to make it cut more effectively and efficiently. To develop your natural gifts and talents (once you've identified them) into strengths requires knowledge and skills (practice).

CHAPTER TWO:
PRINCIPLES

1. If you seek your purpose and pursue it, then you have found God and his blessings, but if not then you are still walking to please yourself.

2. Your purpose is not yours to decide, it is yours to discover.

3. The number one agenda in any man's life is to find out the purpose of God for his or her life and pursue it passionately.

4. The purpose of God in one's life is what puts value on that person's life.

5. A man, who knows his purpose in life, and walks in it, is a very successful man in the sight of God.

6. Accomplishments without purpose are a waste of time.

7. Anytime a gift or talent is being used, its God given purpose should be the focal point of achievement.

8. Purpose is more important to God than importance.

9. Seeking God with all your heart, all of your soul and all of your strength is the secret to finding all of God's purpose for your life.

10. Accomplishments without purpose are a waste of time.

11. Life without a divine purpose is an experiment.

12. Seek God for your destiny and make decisions that agree with that destiny.

13. Destiny has a purpose.

CHAPTER THREE

DEVELOP YOUR GIFTS AND TALENTS

"Seasons of preparation are important to God and to the success of your purpose"

– Joseph Boateng –

In your race through life, do you have all the information and tools you need to express your unique potential and live an extraordinary life before you run out of time, health, love and wisdom? Remember that the gifts and talents you have are in their raw state and must therefore be developed. With the gifts and talents, come special responsibilities for developing and managing them for a God ordained purpose.

Every assignment in life requires a certain period of preparation in order to accomplish it successfully. But also remember that you will never be perfect in this life, because your life as a whole is a work in progress. You are always under construction, so you need to keep developing yourself daily.

With the gifts come special responsibilities for developing and managing them for a God-ordained purpose.

You must always remember to learn and grow and never be corrupted by what you think you know. There will always be something in your life to work on for its improvement. You can be the best you chose to be in your area of assignment as you develop the gifts and talents that match it. It's when you focus totally, intensely, and consistently on your gifts and talents- those gifts and talents that have the potential to payoff - that you have the greatest chance of success."

Paul had this advice for Timothy as a young Minister of the gospel when he said,

> "Neglect not the gift that is in you, which was given (revealed) to you by prophecy, with the laying on of the hands of the presbytery. MEDITATE UPON THESE THINGS; GIVE YOURSELF WHOLLY TO THEM; THAT YOUR PROFITING MAY APPEAR TO ALL. Take heed unto yourself, and unto the doctrine; continue in them: for in doing this you shall both save yourself, and them that hear you". - *1Timothy 4: 14, 15*

As gifted and talented people, we should be constantly seeking to improve our gifts and talents. There are **TWO** important desires that every person must possess, if he or she must become impactful in life.

- **First**: The desire to know more of God - God development (a daily pursuit of God - Be a God chaser).
- **Second:** The desire to improve and become better and effective in whatever you are doing - self (gift & talent) development (a daily pursuit of self - Be a self-developer).

Love yourself (your gifts & talents) so much that, you want it to get better on daily basis. I know of no effective person, who has not sought to excel in whatever he or she is doing, be it preachers, teachers, singers, footballers, etc. Each person should seek to become the best they can in whatever they do. I am amazed at the football talent of Lionel Messi (2015 world footballer of the year), the Argentine who plays for F. C. Barcelona. The truth is that his football skills are not accidental. These are skills which have been developed by continuous practice though he was born with the talent. No matter how gifted you are, there is the need for a continuous practice or development of your gifts and talents to enhance them for greater effectiveness.

ENHANCE YOUR GIFTS & TALENTS FOR EFFECTIVENESS

The development (sharpening) of the gifts and talents is what will make them to work more efficiently and effectively in achieving their purposes. When you identify your gifts and talents and know God's purpose for giving them to you, you must then begin to think of what you can do to develop (sharpen) them. This is what we call, **"the polishing of the gift"**(Eccl 10:10). It is after the gift(s) and talent(s) are well polished or sharpened or developed that you can think of using them to achieve their purposes. Let me ask you? Have you or are you taking the time to develop (polish) your gift(s) and talents? Or you are using them in their raw state. You are your primary instrument, and you must be sharp. Blunt saws don't cut very well.

People are not effective and successful in life or in any business venture, because they have not developed the gifts, talents and abilities given to them by God which has a bearing on their work. Many are so much in a hurry to fulfill their purpose(s) that as soon as they discover their gifts, and talents and the purposes assigned for them, they do not have the patience to develop them.

A wise man said if he were given six hours to weed a plot of land, he would spend four hours (4hrs) sharpening his cutlass and then the rest of the time accomplishing the task. More time and energy should therefore be given to the development of the gifts, talents and abilities you have to enhance them for their effectiveness. Jesus spent thirty years preparing for a three year assignment. He had a thirty year input for a three year output. When you spend more time and effort in the input, you will spend less time and effort in the output to accomplish your assignment. The Bible says that,

> "If the axe is dull, then more strength is required to accomplish a task". - **Ecclesiastes 10:10**

If your gifts and talents are not well polished - that is, if they are still in their raw state, you will spend more energy and effort accomplishing the task at hand which at the end of the day will leave you worn out with little results. Every effort should therefore be invested in the development of the gifts and talents placed within you.

> *Every effort should be invested in the development of the gifts and talents placed within you.*

Until these gifts and talents are well developed, you will never be effective in fulfilling your purpose in life. You must thoroughly complete this dimension of your life before you can really begin to fulfill the purposes for these gifts and talents. Remember that, a dull axe requires great strength; be wise and sharpen the blade.

Why is it that in everyday life, people are willing to sharpen any tool they use, like say a cutlass, a pair of Scissors or a knife to cut something, but are unwilling to sharpen the gifts and talents they have, like say, singing, teaching, preaching, writing, dancing, etc.? They never make the effort to improve themselves in that which they do. They are satisfied with the old way of doing things and are not bothered about mediocrity.

> *Until these gifts and talents are well developed, you will never be effective in fulfilling your purpose in life.*

AN ILLUSTRATION:

Let's consider this illustration in expanding our discussion. Let's take two people for instance who have been given a plot of land to weed. Their purpose is to weed the land. They are each given a cutlass to do the job. But the cutlasses are in their raw state - unsharpened state. One man spends several hours sharpening his cutlass while the other one says he has no time to waste so he goes straight to work. While one is sharpening his cutlass the other one is busy weeding. In about an hours' time, the one weeding looks so exhausted due to his unsharpened cutlass, even at the point of giving up; whiles the other one is now ready to start work with his cutlass well sharpened.

After another one hour, the one who went straight into business without sharpening his cutlass is completely exhausted without any strength to continue because much strength has been exerted, while the one who took time to sharpen his cutlass is enjoying his work. Less strength is been exerted yet with much effectiveness. This situation encourages him to continue to work more and continues to achieve more results from his labor. His labors are not in vain. No wonder Abraham Lincoln said, **"If I had eight hours to chop a tree, I will spend six hours sharpening my axe".**

You must first think of the input before the output, because output flows out of input. If input is good, output will also be good. What you put inside will determine what you get from it (outside). Many people who are not achieving the required results must first sit down and find out whether they have invested the necessary time in developing the gifts, talents and abilities they have. Those who have the gift of say, singing should ask themselves whether they have taken the time to develop the art of singing.

A lot of people want results in what they do, but the question they should ask themselves is whether they have taken the time to develop the gifts and talents they have, for their maximum impact. The problem we have is that we have not taken the time to work upon our gifts and talents to enhance their effectiveness. There are those who think that, the anointing is enough to accomplish any task and so do not see the need for wisdom and understanding in developing their gifts, and talents. They say as long as the anointing comes everything will work out fine.

Whatever we do for God yes requires the anointing but it also requires the development of our gifts and talents. We need not make one suffer for the other. The lack of skills is why we are not getting the results we so desire. There is the place of wisdom and understanding in what we do, which nothing, including prayer or anointing can replace. We need the right skills to succeed in whatever we are doing. It is when the anointing meets preparation (skills) that we will see an explosion in what we do. The Bible says that,

> "A man who is skilled in his work will certainly stand before kings and not ordinary men" - **Proverbs 22:29**

Skillfulness in what we do is what sets us apart from ordinary performance. The import of this passage is this: We should not settle for mediocrity; nor settle for second best, but rather, seek excellence. Why? That we may stand before "kings". You say, "That sounds prideful". No, it's not. The whole point king Solomon was making is this: Anybody can stand before the obscure, but not everybody will have the privilege of addressing kings or those in high profile. It will take those with skill and polish in addition to anointing, to get a hearing.

It is said that in his day, Dr. G. Campbell Morgan, a prominent English preacher, often had kings and presidents attend his meetings. Why? He was a man who had worked and fine-tuned the gift that God had given him, and thus, he was heard even by nobles. When King Saul wanted someone skillful to minister to him in song, it was David the shepherd boy who was called. Though anointed, he was also very skillful. He had so developed the skill of playing the harp that it brought him before the king.

Those who take the time to develop their gifts and talents carry what we call the overtaking anointing. They soon overtake those who have not taken the time to develop their gifts and talents. I might remind you further of the Apostle Paul. His background and training was a great asset when he was brought before the rulers of his day. He was skilled to speak before the small and the great.

We will do well to heed their examples. As ambassadors of the king of kings we should strive for the mastery. You don't have to be in haste and think that people are leaving you behind in life, but you must rather think of the preparation needed to become effective in what you do. The success of your future is connected to how prepared you get today. Therefore seasons of preparation are very important to God and to the success of your life and ministry or calling or purpose.

> *The success of your future is connected to how prepared you are today. Therefore, seasons of preparation are very important to God and to the success of your ministry.*

PREPARATION, THE KEY TO BETTER RESULTS

The results that a person produces are the most important thing in whatever we do and it is connected to the depth of preparation one does. Therefore if you are not ready to pay the price in preparation for anything then forget about getting very good or excellent results. Availability is not the important issue here, but availability with proper preparation leading to better results is the point. If you are not sure you can produce the results required, then you don't make yourself available.

There is a common saying that, "When preparation meets opportunity success is inevitable". And Benjamin Disraeli, former British Prime Minister also, puts it this way, "The secret of success is when a man is ready before the opportunity arrives". For the Bible says that, "time and chance happens to them all" (Ecclesiastes 9: 11). Everybody's time and chance will surely come. But the question is, "will you be ready when your time and chance comes"?

> *The secret of success is when a man is ready before the opportunity arrives.*

People can hand you opportunities, but nobody can hand you preparation. Preparation is your sole responsibility. Anyone who wants to have opportunities must first think of the preparation required to meet those opportunities for effective results. It is always the one who is ready before the opportunities arrives who will produce the required results (excellent results).

> *People can hand you opportunities, but nobody can hand you preparation. The secret of success is when a man is ready before the opportunity arrives.*

Listen, my dear one, result is the reason for whatever we are doing. Life is not for fun. Producing excellent results is the fun. "Look for results because people are looking for results and the one producing the result is the one they want to see". Your destiny is in your own hands. It is your amazing creation. People in Jesus Christ's day sought for Him because He gave them the results they needed. The Pharisees were there before Jesus came on the scene, yet many people followed Him because He met their needs. People will always shift camp to where they can get the results they are looking for. If you can't give the people the results they are looking for, you will soon lose your relevance in their lives. That's the bottom line please!

Look for results because people are looking for results and the one producing the results is the one they want to see.

It is not enough to do something for doing sake. It is the same as salt losing its saltiness; the Bible says that, it's trodden under foot and it's good for nothing (Mathew 5: 13). If you can give people the results they need, they don't mind seeing you every second. As long as you produce or make the necessary impact on people with what you do, people would not mind the number of times they see you. People will rather love to see the one producing results. There is no way you can lose your relevance with the people when you give them the results they are looking for. People go to the same restaurant to virtually eat the same kind of food almost every day and yet are not bored; the reason being that, they like the results they get.

Very good and excellent result is the key to staying relevant wherever you are and in whatever you do. If you give people what they cannot get from anywhere else, they are bound to return to you. And to do this you must be committed to a continual preparation in whatever you are doing. Lack of proper preparation produces what we call "rusting" and when you rust you don't deliver well.

> *If you give people what they cannot get from anywhere else, they are bound to return to you.*

It doesn't matter how nice you are as a person, if you don't give people the excellent results they're looking for, they will soon move on to another person who can give it to them. It is not enough to be a people oriented person, you must also be a result oriented person. You must determine to be both. Real life is all about balance in what you do. Yes, in as much as people want relationships they also want the kind of relationships that can provide solutions to their needs. In fact all good relationships are meant to make our lives get better.

Believe it or not, the needs of people and how they can solve them are their major concern. You must therefore do all it takes to produce the kind of results people are looking for. You must always examine the results you are producing. Always remember this: **"People don't really like you, they like the results you produce"**. Therefore: **"No Results – No You"**. Remember that even the money you make is a bi-product of the value you create for the world. "Improve what you offer, and the world will pay you accordingly for it".

> *People don't like you, they like the results you produce, so "No Results – No You".*

When you don't produce the results people are looking for, people will at least tolerate you but will not celebrate you. When people tolerate you, it means that as soon as they get a better option they will move on. In other words, people are not interested in you. They are not interested in me. They are interested in themselves, in finding solutions to their problems – morning, noon and after dinner. If you fail to produce the required results people are looking for, then that's the end of you in whatever you are doing in life.

> *Improve what you offer, and the world will pay you accordingly for it.*

Anyone who produces better or excellent results is not because he or she is a genius, no! Preparation is the key. I cannot but emphasize this point again. Preparation is the key to excellent results! Preparation is the difference between two results. Preparation positions people correctly, and it is often the separation between winning and losing. Therefore, don't sacrifice your preparation time for anything else, for that's your life. There is the need therefore for you to continuously prepare yourself so that you can produce very good and excellent results. The person who produces excellent result means that he's had enough preparation. Hear me, I did not say, "he's better or more gifted or talented", but rather he's more prepared. Preparation is what separates two gifted people.

> *Preparation is what separates two gifted people. It is the difference between two results. It is the key to excellent results.*

The number of times you've been doing something does not matter, it is the results you produce that matters. In this twenty first century, length of service will not be as important as producing excellent results at what you do. Your promotions in life will come readily due to the excellent results you are producing. Long term service without corresponding excellent results will rather lead to a demotion.

In fact, you are three things: Who you were, who you are, and who you are becoming. There must be continues progress in your life affecting what you do in life. Some people strive so hard to "do" something remarkable that they forget it requires that you first "be" something remarkable. Someone put it best who said, "What you are is God's gift to you, but what you make of yourself is your gift to God".

What you are is God's gift to you, but what you make of yourself is your gift to God.

Remember that, great men (people) won't send for you just because you told them your sad story. People really don't care about your sad story. If they ever heard about your sad story, it is pity they will have for you, not favor. They only care about solutions to their needs and if you can provide them with answers then they will remember you and send for your services.

Joseph of Bible fame, thought that Pharaoh's servant whom he met in prison (The Chief cupbearer to Pharaoh), will remember him after he had been reinstated in his position as a cupbearer, because he (Joseph) told him his sad story of how he has been wrongly accused and put in prison for something he did not do. But Joseph was only sent for by the king, when he had an answer to Pharaoh's problems. Having an answer to a problem is what makes way for you in life. People can forget your sad story but they can't forget your excellent results that meet their needs. **(Gen. 40:23; 41:1-15).** You must therefore concentrate on developing your gifts and talents so you can be more ready when you have the opportunity to use them for an excellent result. Remember that God wants to revolutionize your life and the earlier you get yourself ready by developing your gifts and talents the better you will experience it. Get, get, get ready.

Abraham Lincoln, one of the finest presidents of the United States of America once said, **"Life entrusts positions of responsibility only on those who are prepared for them."** This means that life will find a way to create a position of opportunity for those who will work to prepare themselves today for tomorrow. Remember that life knows how to distinguish between those who are prepared and those who are not prepared and to hand them opportunities for their input to manifest their output. If life and God sees that you are prepared, they will agree to offer you an opportunity to do something great for your generation and the generations unborn.

THE POWER OF KNOWLEDGE

Remember that successful men, in all callings, never stop acquiring specialized knowledge related to their major purpose, business, or profession. Those who are not successful usually make the mistake of believing that the knowledge-acquiring period ends when one finishes school. Many modern-day successful and wealthy people are voracious readers; they never stop learning and challenging their minds in the area where their gifts and passion meets. Knowledge must be continually sought after. You're never done learning. But the benefit of having knowledge is to put into practice, otherwise knowledge will not help you. Knowledge which is not used, puffs up (**1Cor 8:1**) - it produces pride and arrogance, but knowledge applied (wisdom) brings success. Knowledge without application is as useless as a car without wheels.

It is not how much you know but what you do with what you know that will bring great change to your life. It is the doing aspect of knowledge that brings progress to one's life. Knowledge is potential power. An education or knowledge only becomes powerful and leads to great wealth when it is organized and applied to life.

TWO WAYS OF LEARNING

- Learning/ studying to amass knowledge.
- Learning/ studying to acquire knowledge for immediate application in one's life.

Learning/studying to amass knowledge only, does not produce results; it does not bring progress to one's life. It is one thing to study and another thing to put into practice what you study. It is the doing of the word that brings profit into one's life. The Bible says that all received the word, but not all the hearers benefited from the word because some did not mixed the word they heard (knowledge) with faith (actions) – Hebrews 4:2. In fact the Bible says that,

> "Not being a HEARER of the word ONLY deceiving ourselves but rather being a DOER of the word."
> - ***James 1:22***

Knowledge should be a weapon for progress and success in life, for the Bible says that;

> "A man of KNOWLEDGE increases in strength"
> - ***Proverbs 24:5***

But if the knowledge received is not used, it becomes a destructive weapon in one's life. Therefore, one effective way of studying is to have a practical approach towards your studies. The question you should always ask yourself is, "How can I apply these truths of information am receiving in my own life"?

One's aim in learning or studying should be, "How to improve in whatever he or she is doing". As one studies, he or she, should look for ways to apply that knowledge received in his or her circumstances of life. In fact, he must aim at progress at all times. He must determine to improve in whatever he or she is doing in life.

The desire to improve and become better and effective in whatever you are doing should overshadow any other desire apart from your desire for more of God. When you do something better than you did it the last time that is the definition of Success. Insist upon succeeding like you insist upon breathing, then nothing can stop you. When you improve what you offer, the world will pay you accordingly for it. As I said earlier on, "The rewards you get is a bi-product of the value you create for the world".

> *The desire to improve and become better and effective in whatever you are doing should overshadow any other desire apart from your desire for more of God.*

The Bible says that, the path of the righteous is as the light of dawn that shines brighter and brighter until the full light of day **(Prov. 4:18).** Whatever you are doing must get better and better in the cause of each day until its full potential is evident to all. The fact of the matter is that, there can be no success without a sound practice or preparation based on the knowledge received. It is practice, practice and practice (the application of the knowledge received), that improves the ability to deliver effectively.

LAZINESS: THE KILLER OF DESTINY (Prov. 6:9-10; 19:15; 24:33)

If you really want to succeed in whatever God has called you to do, then laziness should be far from you. That is, laziness in practicing what you have been called to do or whatever you are doing now, be it preaching, teaching, singing, writing, playing the piano, studying your mathematics as a student or any other assignment etc. You can be a very gifted person but if you don't practice your gift or work, you will not be effective.

> *If you really want to succeed in whatever God has called you to do, then laziness should be far from you. Laziness in practicing or preparation.*

Laziness is not the absence of work, but it is rather the absence of the required effort needed to make something work the way it should. It is not just putting in some effort but the required effort. There is always the required effort needed to make something work the way it should. Practice is what makes one perfect and permanent in what he does. Until you put into practice what you have learnt or been taught, you cannot get the benefits it promises. Some are just lazy in what they do. They just sit and waste precious time they could have used to develop their skill in what they do be it mathematics, biology, chemistry, singing, preaching, teaching etc.

GOD'S PREPARATORY SCHOOL

Apart from you taking the responsibility to develop your gifts and talents, God has his own kind of preparation he takes every individual he has called through which is meant to develop godly character in them. Excellent character is the bedrock for any excellent life. The reason why we have many casualties in the body of Christ is that, many have not finished their preparatory school within God's stipulated time. Many are ill-prepared and so, instead of triumphing over life situations, they have become casualties. Many have gone ahead of God when they should be behind and have therefore received hard knocks they have not been prepared for and thereby have broken 'jaws'. Some have even lost the enthusiasm and zeal for life due to the hard knocks of life because they are ill-prepared.

The circumstances of life have had their toll on them. They have lost their joy and strength to continue on the journey of life. The bible says that, "If you fail in time of adversity then your strength is small".

> *Until you finish God's preparatory school, you will not be able to face life situations and triumph over them.*

It takes a lot of patience to continue in God's Preparatory School, because sometimes the tests involved are difficult. But you can be very sure that after you have gone through the school, you will begin to have dominion over life situations. God's Preparatory School is the best school in the whole world. Every student that has ever come out of it has emerged with a successful record in life situations.

There is no way you can come out of God's Preparatory School and fail in life situations. Remember that God does not produce failures; He always produces champions. If anyone desires to be a champion in life, he should therefore have the courage and patience to stay in God's Preparatory School.

> *If anyone desires to be a champion in life, let him therefore have the courage and patience to stay in God's Preparatory School.*

In God's preparatory school, all your dependency on people – that is, your family, friends, etc. will be stopped. In fact, you will be changed from human dependent into God dependent. Everything you need will be supplied by the school authorities (the Father, the Son and the Holy Spirit). Any other sources of supply will be terminated and you will have to only depend on the school authorities to supply all your needs. You will have to trust God to supply your needs according to his riches in glory in Christ Jesus. One main criterion for graduating from God's Preparatory School is to be completely dependent on God (the school authorities) for all your needs. This is how you will know that your preparation is nearing completion. Yes it is possible to graduate from a human institution and still not graduate from God's Preparatory School.

> *One main criterion for graduating from God's preparatory school is to be completely dependent on the school authorities for all your needs.*

As long as you continue to depend on, or trust in or rely on any other sources of supply other than God, then know that your graduation day is far from you. Remember that some of these sources of supply may be your parents, brothers, sisters, friends or any other person you have been depending on all your life, and this will require a strong trust in God to dissociate yourself from their influences. The reason for this is that; if you continue to trust man for your needs to be met then you are no longer in God's Preparatory School but in man's preparatory school. Know that man's preparatory school is not good enough to prepare you to face the kind of life situations that will come to you because of your kind of calling or purpose.

Those prepared from man's preparatory school are full of complaining and murmuring. When they face life situations, they easily give up and are therefore defeated. Students from man's preparatory school always compromises when they meet opposing situations. They are full of excuses and therefore do not follow the will of God through and through. They are men pleasers and not God pleasers. They seek men's approval instead of God's approval. They are more concerned about what men will say to them and about them than what God is saying to them.

God most times wants to shut a door that will not lead you to his purpose for your life completely before He can open doors to new possibilities. Maybe you have had some doors close in your life. In spite of everything, know that God is stirring you to accomplish His purpose in your life. God knows what it takes to bring order back to your life. Trust Him. He's working on something and when He's done, everything around you will be made better.

> *If you are still trusting man for your needs to be met, then you are no longer in God's Preparatory School but in man's preparatory school.*

Example of compromisers, complainers and murmurs were the people of Israel when they were in the wilderness towards the Promised Land. These were people who always looked back to Egypt (to human help) when they were faced with difficult situations. They always looked back to where they had depended for their daily need. Instead of trusting God to meet their needs, they rather complained and murmured against God and His servant Moses.

They had lived all their lives in Egypt depending on them for their daily needs and could not dissociate themselves from them. They needed a strong faith in God to enable them to know that God was able to meet their needs. The Bible says that,

> "And when they came to Marah, they could not drink of the waters of Marah, for they were bitter: therefore the name of it was called Marah. And the people murmured against Moses, saying, what we shall drink". - **Exodus 15:23-24**

As for complaints and murmurings, it became the order of the day for many of them. The Bible says again that,

> And the children of Israel said unto them, would to God we had died by the hand of the Lord in the land of Egypt, when we sat by the flesh pots, and when we did eat bread to the full; for ye have brought us forth into this wilderness, to kill this whole assembly with hunger. - **Exodus 16:3**

Students who have passed through God's Preparatory School are always loyal to the school authorities and are very faithful. We have many examples of students who have graduated from God's Preparatory School and the results they achieved in life situations. God's preparatory School is the best school; the standard of living is very high; commitment and hard work are their hall mark.

Where are you in your walk with God? Probably you are in God's preparatory school and sometimes its feels you cannot make it, but, trust me, if you will look up to God, you will come out and triumph over life situations and possess your inheritances.

> *God's Preparatory School is the best school; the standard of living is very high; Commitment and hard work are their hall mark.*

DESERT TIME IS PREPARATION TIME

God will always prepare His people before He puts them in front of battle to face the enemy, or give them opportunities to advance them, so they can possess their promised land (inheritance). Though God has given us great promises and the assurance to help us for our total victory in life situations, we on our part need to have faith in Him. God will always take you through situations and challenges in order to build up your faith in Him for the victories he has promised you. The Bible says that,

The Israelites:

> "When Pharaoh Let the people go, God did not lead them on the road through the Philistine country, though that was shorter. For God said, "If they face war, they might change their minds and return to Egypt. So God led the people around about the desert road toward the red sea. The Israelites went up out of Egypt armed for battle".
> - ***Exodus 13:17-18 NIV***

The Bible says that, the Israelites were armed for battle, but they were not yet ready (prepared) for battle. God had given them great and wonderful promises but they had to be fully prepared to do a good warfare in order to possess them. They needed to be strong and bold on the inside of them, if they were to face their enemies and overcome them. An unwavering confidence in God is what they require if they were to conquer their enemies. They had to walk with God in order to experience and to develop their faith in Him. God had to take them through the wilderness, so that life in the wilderness will allow them to see the power of God; which was to help develop their confidence in Him and not in themselves. This was to enable them face their enemies and possess the Promised Land when the time came. Though God designed the wilderness time to be their preparation time, many of them did not allow themselves to be trained and prepared by God through their circumstances and so failed to enter into the promise land.

Lack of preparation prevents people from stepping into what God has promised them. Those who are unprepared see opportunities as oppositions and therefore miss their day of visitation.

Those who are unprepared see opportunities as opposition and therefore miss the day of their visitation.

Whiles ten out of the twelve spies saw entering the Promised Land as opposition, the two left (Joshua and Caleb) saw it as an opportunity to step into the next phase of their lives. The twelve spies all went through the same wilderness experience and yet ten were not ready except two. Two had followed Moses (God) with all of their heart regardless of their circumstances, but the ten had been part of those who had followed God, but were full of complains and murmurings.

When you murmur and complain you deny yourself the opportunity to be trained and prepared. Complaining and murmuring means you are against the training and preparation you are undergoing. It means you hate even the trainer who is preparing you for the day of your lifting (Promotion). How then do you expect to be ready when the time comes for your lifting? Such people don't even recognize the day of their visitation because they see it as opposition and will even resist it. The Bible says that, "Humble yourselves in the presence of the Lord, and He will exalt you in due time" (James 4:10). Your preparation is a must and there is no short cut to that.

> *An unwavering confidence in God is what is required, if one must to conquer his or her enemies and recover what belongs to him/her.*

David:

Actually, the Bible gives us more details about the life of David than any other person with the possible exception of Paul in the New Testament. From the accounts in the books of Samuel and Chronicles plus some of the Psalms ascribed to David, we learn that David was a multifaceted individual with great gifts and talents and abundant charm. Some of his abilities seem to have been endowed by God, and others he learned and developed by his disciplined behavior.

We first met David as the youngest of eight sons of Jesse. David may well have been the "runt of the litter," and we are told that he had fair complexion and light red hair. He was quite obviously, the unappreciated "baby brother" of the household, and he was assigned the task of tending the family's flock of sheep. Rather than lament or complain that he had been virtually thrust out of his home to live with the sheep, David used those long days and nights of loneliness to sharpen his skills with his slingshot and to teach himself to play the simple one or two stringed shepherd's harp he had made. This was the beginning of his musical career that would touch the lives of his generation and succeeding generations until the present.

It was also during this period of minimal responsibility that David came to know God so intimately. Long nights under the stars lifted David's thoughts far above his mundane shepherd's life, and he could cry,

> *"When I consider your heavens, the work of your fingers, the moon and the stars, which you have ordained, what is man that you are mindful of him, and the son of man that you visit him?"* - **Psalm 8:3-4**

It seems consistent that the persons who get the "lucky breaks" are also the persons who discipline themselves to use "idle time" to develop their gifts and talents. Moses and Paul needed seasons of solitude in the desert, and David too profited greatly by his lengthy season of solitude while the sheep chewed their cud. Some of us never learn that "desert" time is preparation time.

> *It seems consistent that the persons who get the "lucky breaks" are also the persons who discipline themselves to use "idle time" to develop their gifts & talents.*

It was David's musical skill that first brought him to the attention of King Saul, and this youthful shepherd's ability to use a slingshot skyrocketed him to Israel's attention. He eventually married into the royal family as an outgrowth of these two developed gifts and talents. He also developed other capabilities. He proved himself to be a great organizer with an uncanny capacity to recognize a person's ability and to assign that person to the place for which he or she was fitted. He was a fair and faithful King, who with the only exception of forcing a census upon unwilling nation and impregnating someone's wife, never used his power and authority for personal and selfish ends. He was generous, he was just, and he was always approachable. Politically, he was shrewd and far-seeing, and his military skill gave him victory in all his wars. David was passionately a patriot of Israel, though his great-grandmother, Ruth was Moabite.

> Some of us never learn that "desert" time is preparation time.

Joseph:

Although God had revealed to Joseph the purpose for his life, he had to go through his desert time to be fully prepared by God. His gifts and talents which would be needed to fulfill his destiny had to be properly developed for their effective use. His management and leadership skills brought him before Potiphar. The Bible says that his master Potiphar completely left the day to day running of his house in the hands of Joseph. This responsibility to manage Potiphar's house gave Joseph the opportunity to sharpen his managerial skills. This ability to lead and manage successful enterprises' made him a leader even in prison.

His gift of interpretation of dreams brought him before Pharaoh's former stewards who were also in prison. This same gift finally brought him before Pharaoh and made him the prime minister of Egypt. His managerial skills and his ability to interpret dreams which is seen as wisdom, qualified him as the manager of the resources of Egypt.

Everything Joseph went through from when he was sold till when he became a prime minister of Egypt was preparation for the final promotion God had shown him in his dreams. All the things that happened to him were all meant to work together for his good towards the purpose of God for his life. The secret to his success, was the fact that God was with him and his willingness not to compromise his relationship with God. God will help you to succeed as you follow him diligently with all your heart.

PREPARATION IS CONNECTED TO YOUR PURPOSE

Your kind of preparation is connected to your kind of purpose in life. The purpose for which God created you will determine the kind of preparation you go through in life. In life, you have people going through different experiences, which at the end, work together for good towards God's purposes for their lives. In God's preparatory school, you have people going through their major preparation section within different periods of times.

> *Your kind of preparation is connected to your kind of purpose in life.*

ILLUSTRATION:

Let us consider a group of students who enter the university the same year but are offering different courses. Some of the students due to the nature of the course, lets say, engineering students, are supposed to complete their course in four years (4yrs) and their counterparts who are offering medicine are supposed to complete their course in seven to eight years (7-8yrs). The medical students who are completing their course in 7-8yrs, are doing so not because they are dummy or very important people, but it is due to the nature of the course they are offering. The nature of the course you've been offered or you have chosen to do, is what will determine the nature and duration of the preparation you go through. It is therefore out of ignorance that people compare themselves and even compete with one another.

> *It is out of ignorance that people compare themselves with others.*

The Bible says that,

> "We do not dare to classify or compare ourselves with some who commend themselves. When they measure themselves by themselves and compare themselves with themselves, they are not wise". - **2 Corinthians 10:12**

You must move on in life because of the purpose of your calling and not because of the people around you. Your purpose in life will determine how deep and how long it takes you to go through these seasons of preparation that God will allow you to go through and this can only be told you by the one who gave you the purpose in the first place. It is not the student who determines how long he or she will take to finish his or her course (training); it is the school authorities that determine that.

You should remember that a successful performance of your duties as far as your purpose in life is concerned, is connected to how well you complete your preparation within the required duration. Do not forget that it is only God who can truly tell when you have successfully completed your preparation in His school.

> *The successful performance of your duties as far as your purpose in life is concerned, is connected to how well you complete your preparation.*

CHAPTER THREE:
PRINCIPLES

1. Seasons of preparation are important to God and to the success of your ministry, calling or purpose.

2. Your gifts and talents are in their raw state and must therefore be developed.

3. Every effort should be invested in the development of the gifts and talents placed within you.

4. The desire to improve and become better and effective in whatever you are doing should overshadow any other desire apart from your desire for more of God. (This is very important).

5. If you want to succeed in what God has called you to do then laziness should be far from you.

6. The secret to success is when a man is ready before the opportunity arrives.

7. If you give people what they cannot get from anywhere else, they are bound to return to you.

8   Look for results because people are looking for results.

9   Remember that people don't like you, they like the results you produce. Therefore No Results – No You.

10 Preparation is what separates two gifted people. It is the difference between two results.

11 Your kind of preparation is connected to your kind of purpose in life

12 Seasons of preparation are important to God and the success of your purpose in life.

13 The successful performance of your duties as far as your purpose in life is concerned, is connected to how well you complete your preparation within the required duration.

14 What you are is God's gift to you, but what you make of yourself is your gift to God.

15 Destiny has steps.

CHAPTER FOUR

GOD'S WAY OF FULFILLING YOUR DESTINY

"When you do things in the right time, in the right season and with the right purpose — God will surely bless you"
- *T. D Jakes* -

"The Holy Spirit time is the right time."
- *Joseph Boateng* -

Every body's harvest or fruitfulness in life is directly connected to where God has placed them according to His purpose. It is laziness that makes one think that until he goes to some special place or gets someone special to help, he cannot become what he or she desires.

Planning coupled with hard work (action) is all you need to start from where you are towards where you want to get to in life. Therefore don't be afraid or feel alone, but with God on your side, as you pursue your purpose and dreams, enlargement will come.

> *Planning coupled with hard work (taking steps) is all you need to start from where you are towards where you want to get to in life according to your purpose.*

Everyone who has a plan easily encounters opportunities. There are many opportunities but because people don't have any plan those opportunities pass them by without them even knowing it. Remember that, you will always be looked down upon when you start pursuing your divine purpose in life (Neh. 4:4). For people value you according to what they can see physically around you, like having a car, wearing a nice fashionable dress, nice quality pair of shoe etc., but your real value is what you have on the inside of you (your gifts and talents for a divine purpose) put there by God. God always goes all out for whosoever that rises up to do something about what he has placed in him or called him to do.

Don't compare yourself with anyone else. You may be tempted to do as other people are doing. God's plan for you is different, and the way to everyone's harvest is not the same. Concentrate on your path towards your harvest. Someone's path to his harvest might be the path to your famine and shame. Be very sensitive during your harvest time so you can focus on the way that leads to your harvest. There are specific instructions to specific individuals on how to enter their harvest in life when the right time comes. God will surely guide and lead you in the way that you should go into profiting.

WHAT TIME IS THE RIGHT TIME?
THE HOLY SPIRIT TIME IS THE RIGHT TIME!

You may ask, when is the right time to do the things God has placed in your heart to do for him? The answer is: "The Holy Spirit time is the right time". God's time is the best as we always say. Destiny has time. Remember that man's right time is not God's right time. The Bible says that,

> "He has made everything beautiful in His time" - **Eccl. 3:11a**

There is a time called God's time and until that time is known, every right thing we embark on will experience frustration or failure. It is the ability of walking in God's timing that command success in every adventure we take. Jesus understood that man's time is not God's time and that, it is only when he walks in God's timing that he will see the glory of God in his life and ministry. He did not allow anybody to influence him. He rather made sure he influenced those who came to him according to God's purpose for his life; whether it was the Pharisee, the Sadducees or the general public. The Bible says that,

> "And when they had found him, they said unto him, all men seek you. And he said unto them; let us go into the next towns that I may preach there also: for this purpose came I forth". - **Mark 1:37-38**

He did not respond to the demands of the people but rather he went on to do the purpose for his coming to the earth. Some things may look urgent and yet not be important as far as the will of

God is concerned for your life. Urgent things always act on us and if we don't have a strong yes on the inside of us for the purpose of God that He has called us to do, we will waste precious time on unimportant things. The urgent things are always the selfish needs and concerns and opinions of people whiles the important things are the things God is prompting us to do according to His perfect will for our lives. Yes, all the people were looking for Jesus probably for him to solve their selfish needs. The people were looking for Jesus not because of who He was but for what He could do for them. They were more concerned with their selfish needs.

He told them, in effect, "I know why you're here. You aren't looking for me; you're looking for a blessing. You're looking for more free fish and bread." The fact that Jesus had answers to the needs of people, didn't mean, they could just bump into his life and interrupt the will of God (purpose) for his day. They were only interested in what they could get out of him and not their genuine interest in knowing Him and the will of God for their lives.

When Peter and the other disciples found him (Jesus), they exclaimed, *"Everyone is looking for you"*. Jesus could have basked in the people's praise, but he continued to follow His life's purpose. God had shown Him the next step when He was in prayer. He said, "Let us go to the next village, so I can preach there also, **"THAT IS WHY I HAVE COME"**. Do you know why you have come on this earth? Then stay focused in fulfilling it without distractions from the circumstances surrounding you.

> "The Holy Spirit time is the right time"

Jesus was also not influenced by the comments of his own town folks or his family when he went to visit them. For them it was as usual, another time of the feast, but for Jesus, he had a purpose to fulfill and it must be within God's timing. The people had become very legalistic with their feast of celebrations. They were punctually obeying the time to go to their feast. But for Jesus it was not business as usual, he was on the earth to do the bidding of the father and it was important he listens to the instructions of God and not the customs or traditions of the times. If He must receive divine help or divine backing then he must walk in God's timing. The Bible says that,

> *"Then Jesus said unto them, my time is not yet come: but your time is always ready. Go you up unto this feast: I go not up yet unto this feast; for my time is not yet full come."*
> *- **John 7: 6 & 8***

It is the ability of walking in God's timing that commands cheap success in every adventure we take in life. Jesus did not even want to be an hour ahead or behind, but rather wanted to be on time. The Holy Spirit time is the right time. Be therefore in step with the Holy Spirit.

> *It is the ability of walking in God's timing that commands cheap success in every adventure we undertake.*

DON'T BE MOVED BY WHAT YOU SEE OR HEAR

One major quality of a successful life is the quality of not been easily influenced by natural circumstances - like the comments by people (what people say), expressions on people's faces, opinions of people, the concerns and needs of people. In short, be not influenced by man, but be rather influenced by God and led by the Holy Spirit.

> *One major quality of a successful life is the quality of not being easily influenced by natural circumstances.*

The Bible says concerning Jesus, that the Holy Spirit will make Him of quick understanding in the fear of the Lord, which will cause him not to judge by what he sees neither reprove by what he hears. He will only act by the leadings of the Holy Spirit.

> *"And shall make him of quick understanding in the fear of the LORD: and he shall not judge after the sight of his eyes, neither reprove after the hearing of his ears." -* **Isa. 11:3**

There was a day in the life of Jesus and His ministry when he received a call that the one whom he loved (Lazarus) was sick near unto death and yet Jesus was not influenced by such news as far as what to do and when to do it was concerned (John 11:1-14). The scriptures says that,

> "When he had heard therefore that he was sick, HE ABODE TWO DAYS STILL in the SAME PLACE where he was. Then after that he says to his disciples, let us go into Judea again." - **John 11:6-7**

Naturally, it is so easy to be moved straightaway by such news, especially when it concerns a loved one and you know there is something you can do about it. Even if you cannot do anything about it, you will just want to still go around to show your concern and sympathy.

That quality that Jesus had, which enabled him not to be influenced by such news even though they were one family he was close to and rather waited till he received the go ahead signal from the father through the Holy Spirit as to what to do and when to do it, is what we all need if we must see the glory of God in our lives and ministries (divine assignments). The manifestation of the glory of God is always connected to God's own time.

> *"The manifestation of the glory of God is always connected to God's own time".*

Doing the right thing at God's time and God's way is what will produce the right results. Jesus only did what he saw the father do. He did nothing of himself. So He said,

> *"Verily, verily I say unto you, the son can do nothing of himself, but what he sees the father do; for what things so ever he (the father) does, these also does the son likewise".*
> **- John 5:19**

That is why 1 Peter 5:6 says that, **"Humble yourself therefore under the mighty hand of God, that he may exalt you in due time.** There is the need therefore for everyone to be conscious of this right time of God, so that we can get the maximum results from every step we take in life and ministry. The tragedy of the matter is that we are so easily influenced by the natural circumstances that surrounds us that we are easily moved to react to situations and move out of the will or timings of God for our lives.

Any time you react to situations, you lose control of the situation. The situation will rather control you. It is only when you act based on the directions or convictions coming from your heart by the Holy Spirit that will you control the situation. Any time you react to situations, you are being controlled, but any time you act, you are in control. You act because you know the right thing to do but when you react it's because you don't know the right thing to do and you are just trying your luck.

The Bible says that, "And Jesus asked the disciples where they will get food to feed the people who had come to hear the word of God. Though He asked them, the Bible says, He knew what He will do. He was not going to react not knowing what to do. He knew what He will do. And because He knew exactly what He will do, He had the situation under control. The disciples did not know what to do and so in their reaction the situation controlled them. But for Jesus, "He himself knew what He will do". When you walk closely with the Holy Spirit, He will help you to know what to do in every situation.

Any time you react to situations, you are being controlled, whiles any time you act, you are in control.

The willingness to wait for God's timing is not an easy thing for man especially the natural man. Waiting is not pleasant for man at all, but having understanding of being on the right path or being in the will of God, empowers one to stay put till God brings an opportunity (opens a door) to take you forward towards your desired destination. Sometimes all that will be required of you is to wait for God's timing. It is better to wait on the right path than to move on the wrong path.

Many people in the midst of challenges have moved into doors that led them away from the perfect will of God for their lives. Until we are willing and obedient to follow God whole heartedly no matter what, we will move into wrong doors that do not take us to Gods destined places for us.

The willingness to wait for God's timing is not an easy thing for man especially the natural man.

We have people at different stages in life as far as the will of God for their lives is concerned.

- We have those who are waiting on the wrong path concerning God's purpose for them; they have no idea of what God has destined for them. They are not in God's will for their lives at all.

- We also have those waiting on the right path to their destiny; they might not be moving forward now or making much progress but they are in the will of God for their life. They might be under construction or work in progress.

- We also have those moving on the wrong path in life. They are indeed doing something in life but they are totally on their own, far from what God has ordained for them to be or do.

- We also have those moving on the right path to their destiny. These people know the purpose of God for their lives and are in step with God's timing fulfilling that purpose.

Moving therefore is not the most important thing, but whether you are moving on the right path to your divine destination. One needs a lot of patient walk with God if one must successfully fulfill the purpose of God for the gifts and talents he or she has.

> One need a lot of patient walk with God if one must successfully fulfill the purpose of God for the gifts and talents he/she has.

BEING STRENGTHENED WITH MIGHT BY HIS SPIRIT

We need to be tough on the inside of us in order not to be influenced so quickly and easily by the circumstances that surrounds us. Being tough on the inside of us helps us to walk in the right timing and path of God.

> *Being tough on the inside helps you to walk in the right timing and path of God.*

The life of Saul, the first King of Israel illustrates what I am sharing with you. Let us consider the scriptures below,

> *"And he tarried seven days, according to the **set time** Samuel had appointed: but Samuel came not to Gilgal; and the people were scattered from him. And Saul said, Bring hither a burnt offering to me, and peace offering. And he offered the burnt offering. And it came to pass, **as soon as** he had made an end of offering the burnt offering, behold, Samuel came; and Saul went out to meet him that he might salute him. And Samuel said what hast thou done? And Saul said, because I saw that **the people** were scattered from me, and that you came not within the days appointed, and that the Philistines gathered themselves together at Michmash: Therefore said I, the Philistines will come down now upon me to Gilgal, and I have not made supplication unto the Lord: **I forced myself** therefore, and offered a burnt offering. And Samuel said to Saul, Thou hast done foolishly: Thou*

> hast not kept the commandments of the Lord thy God, which he commanded thee: For now would the Lord have established thy Kingdom upon Israel forever. But now thy kingdom shall not continue: The Lord hath sought him a man after his own heart, and the Lord hath commanded him to be captain over his people, because thou hast not kept that which the Lord commanded you".
> - *1 Samuel 13:8-14*

The above passage talks about Saul the first King of Israel. One day he was to go to war against the people of Philistine. Normally before the people of Israel or kings go to war they will first have to make certain sacrifices to their God and seek his guidance and help concerning the war. It was always the duty of the Prophets or the priests to make those sacrifices. One of the duties of the king was to lead the army to war. The king was the chief army commander. It was not the duty of the kings to perform these sacrifices and rituals. King Saul was waiting for the Prophet Samuel to come and perform those sacrifices or rituals and to seek God for his direction before they would go to this war.

The Bible says he waited for Samuel and it looked as if he wasn't coming and the fact that his people also were leaving him for fear of the Philistine, he reacted foolishly outside of the will of God. He forced himself and offered the sacrifice which wasn't his responsibility to offer. King Saul was so easily influenced by what he heard and saw around him that he reacted foolishly. It takes our strong faith in God to give us the inner fortitude to stand still to know what God is saying and act accordingly in order to see the results He has promised us. Bible says that, "he forced himself" to disobey the commandments of the Lord out of fear. People who lack faith in God are full of fear and it is fear that makes us react to the challenging situations around us. King Saul allowed the external pressures to make him do the wrong thing.

This act of disobedience caused him his life and his kingdom. His ministry was gone. The fact of the matter is that, we are not supposed to force ourselves to do anything for God. When times are hard, the people will always run away, but you the leader must not fret but wait on God for his timing and directions. If we do anything in haste outside of the will of God for our lives, we will fail. This is exactly what happened to King Saul.

> *We are not supposed to force ourselves to do anything for God.*

In contrast to how Saul behaved, there was a day in the life of David and his army, when their enemies came and captured all their wives and children and took all their properties away and burnt their houses when they were out in battle. All the mighty men of David wept when they came back and saw what had happened to their families. They wept until they had no strength in them to weep and wanted to even stone David for what had happened to their families and properties. Since David was the one who led them to go to war, they blamed him for their misfortune. This is what the scriptures says,

> *"When David and his men came to Ziklag, they found it destroyed by fire and their wives and their sons and daughters taken captives. So David and his men wept aloud until they had no strength left to weep. David's two wives had been captured- Ahinoam of Jezreel and Abigail, the widow of Nabal of Carmel. David was greatly distressed because the men were talking of stoning him; each one was bitter in spirit because of his sons and daughters. David found strength in the LORD his God. Then David said to Abiathar the priest, the son of Ahimelech, "Bring me the ephod." Abiathar brought it to him, and David inquired of the LORD, "Shall I pursue this raiding party? Will I overtake them?" Pursue them, "he answered. You will certainly overtake them and succeed in the rescue."*
> *- 1 Samuel 30:3-8*

The Bible said that while the men of David where reacting to the situation, David encouraged himself in the Lord and sought the face of the Lord for his instructions and directions. He did not fret. He did not allow the situation to make him take any hasty decision. He refused to react to the situation as his people were doing. He refused to allow the external pressures from his people to make him take any hasty decision. He as their leader waited on God for his instructions and advice. God then instructed him to pursue the enemies and promised him a recovery of all that they had stolen from them.

He received assurance from the Lord of his total support of victory over the enemies and a recovery of all that the enemy had stolen from them. David acted based on divine directions rather than react based on the physical circumstances he saw with his eyes. This is where the victory over life challenges lies.

> *When you act you take charge of the situation. You can only act when you do the right thing and doing the right thing is when it's done in God's timing and in his way.*

David acted rather than react to the situation. When you act you take charge of the situation. You can only act when you do the right thing and doing the right thing is when it's done in God's timing and his way. David had a choice to fret and react foolishly in the face of such a situation, but he trusted in God to help him find the right solution to the problem. Faith in God is the key to victories in life challenges. Fear leads us to failure whiles faith leads us to victory. Some trust in chariots and horses but those who trust in God will see the victory over life challenges. The degree of our victories in life and ministry is connected to the degree of instructions and directions we receive from the Spirit of God especially in times of challenges. The ability to wait on God for his timing and directions requires strength (faith) on the inside of us, so we are not easily distracted by the things we see and hear around us. The man who is easily influenced by natural things, will not enjoy the privilege of being influence by spiritual things (by the Holy Spirit).

> *The man who is easily influenced by natural things will not enjoy the privilege of being influenced by the Holy Spirit.*

That is why Paul prayed for the Ephesians' church,

> *"That God would grant you, according to the riches of his glory, to be strengthened with might by his Spirit in the inner man."* - **Ephesians 3: 10**

Paul's desire was to pray for his followers so that they will be strengthened with might in the inner man by the Holy Spirit, so they can follow God's timing and do his perfect will. Man is naturally concerned with a lot of natural things and these things have a pull on him. Until toughness is developed on the inside through confident trust in God, man will be easily distracted by the challenges of life. The needs of your family, friends, people in your community and opinions of people have a great deal of potential to distract you if you are not strong on the inside. How easily you are influenced by natural things is an indication of how weak you are on the inside of you. Spiritual things are superior to natural things. The natural came out of the spiritual. Without the spiritual, the natural will lose its essence of existence.

> *How easily you are influenced by natural things, is an indication of how weak you are on the inside of you.*

The Bible says concerning Christ Jesus that,

> "He shall not judge after the sight of his eyes, neither reprove after the hearing of his ears" - **Isaiah 11:3b**

Jesus did not make decisions based on what he saw with his natural eyes nor on what he heard with his natural ears. He made decisions when it was the right thing to do and it was right only when God the father through the Holy Spirit said it was so. It didn't matter who said what, if it didn't agree with the will or purpose of God, then it was not right. It is therefore not every good thing that you must respond to; you are only to respond to the ones God is commanding you.

Many have entered into very good ventures and yet have failed miserably because God never asked them to do it in the first place or even if God asked them to do it, the **when** and the **how** to do it was not known or followed.

HEAVENLY STRENGTH FOR HEAVENLY VISION

Earthly (human) strength can never accomplish a heavenly (divine) vision or purpose. Any heavenly vision revealed to you by God can only be fulfilled by heavenly strength. Any God sent vision will be accompanied with a God sent strength for its accomplishment. This is why Apostle Paul said in the book of Philippians that,

> "Being confident of this, that he, who has begun a good work in you and with you, will carry it on to completion until the day of Jesus Christ." - **Philippians 1:6**

No one can of himself complete the work that God has begun with him or her. The hand that begins is the same hands that will and must complete. Since God's hands are stronger than man's hand, it will be a suicidal mission to try to complete what God has begun, with the feeble hands of man. Remember that what God always begins to do with a man is always bigger than the man, and so can only be accomplished with the strength of God. So never attempt to take over what God has begun doing in your life; allow God by trusting him to complete what He has started with you.

> *Never attempt to take over what God has begun doing in your life.*

The Bible says that, "**It does not, therefore, depend on man's desire or effort, but on God who shows mercy (Romans 9:16).**

Any time you feel too weak to bear up under the challenges that life's brings your way or you feel inadequate to face life test, it should remind you of God's strength available to help you accomplish the task ahead. Until you see your weaknesses in the face of the task ahead, you will not experience the strength of God. God's strength flows in the direction of our weaknesses. Strength can only replace weakness. Strength will always struggle with strength; divine strength will conflict with human strength.

The easiest way to experience the strength of God is when you genuinely see your weakness or inadequacies in the face of the task ahead and trust God for his strength. The task God has for us will always be more challenging than we can handle by our human strength, but that should remind us of God's help available for us. The Bible says that, **"My grace is sufficient for you: for my strength is made perfect in your weakness" (2 Corinthians 12:9).**

The Bible also says that,

> *"Do you not know? Have you not heard? The LORD is the everlasting God, the creator of the ends of the earth. He will not grow tired or weary, and his understanding no one can fathom. He gives strength to the weary, and increases the power of the weak. Even youths grow tired and weary, and young men stumble and fall; but those who hope in the LORD will renew their strength. They will soar on wings like eagles; they will run and not grow weary, they will walk and not be faint".* **- Isaiah 40:28-31**

There is the need to fellowship with the Spirit of God, if you must enjoy his strength for greater works. This strength is what we call the hand of the Lord which produces in you what we call the inner strength which knows no faintness or weariness. It empowers you to fulfill the assignment given to you by God. It makes you to go the extra mile that ordinary human strength cannot go.

DEVELOPING THE MINDSET TO BE A BLESSING

Until the needs of people become the driving force for all you do, you will not be a blessing to anyone in this life. The question you should always ask yourself is this: "why am I doing what I'm doing"? Until you answer this question correctly and sincerely, you are not ready to succeed in whatever endeavor you undertake.

Whatever you have is because of the benefit of people. Anytime you have a need, the first thing to do is to find out how you can become a blessing to the people around you and not how you can have your needs met. Your needs will only be met when you do something genuinely to meet the needs of someone else. The more you become pre-occupied with your own needs, the more you stay in your needs. What a man sows is what he will reap also.

If you want to be blessed, don't focus on your needs; rather, discover what the other person needs are and seek to fulfill them. This approach will become a double blessing, because consistently meeting the needs of another person will often cause that person to want to fulfill yours. Whenever you are not receiving what you need in a relationship, evaluate whether you have been trying to meet the other person's needs first. Giving to others by satisfying their needs – not demanding to have our own needs satisfied – will bring true fulfillment.

Until what you do for people springs from a genuine desire to see their well-being, you will become a burden instead of a blessing.

The whole issue about this life is not about having your needs met, but rather meeting the needs of people. You will always have to use what you have to solve the problems of people first, before you can get what you need. Your motive should not be what you can get, but what you can give to make a difference in the lives of people. A real passion to help people in their problems is the gateway to a successful life.

A real passion to help people in their problems is the gateway to a successful life.

Instead of asking of how you can have your needs met, you should rather ask how you can meet the need(s) of the people around you. You will only live when you make others live. Your existence is based on the existence of the other people around you. It is only when you carry the giving mentally that what you have (the anointing, wisdom, counsel, knowledge, etc.) can flow to become a blessing to people. People mostly think of giving in terms of money, but giving has to do with whatever you can offer people to meet a need. For this reason, people who don't have physical cash look down on themselves as not having anything to offer mankind.

In the book of Acts something happened there that I will want to use to illustrate my point. Peter and John went up together to the temple to pray. They met this lame man who always sat at the entrance of the temple and beg for alms. Who, seeing Peter and John about to go into the temple, asked for alms. Whiles the lame man was expecting to receive some money from them, Peter said to him, **"Silver and gold I do not have, but what I do have I give you: In the name of Jesus Christ of Nazareth, rise up and walk" (Acts 3:6)**.

Peter in a sense said, we don't have money at the moment to give you, but there is something else we have which is relevant to meet a need in your life. Not having money doesn't make you useless in the affairs of this life. Jesus did not give money to the disciples when he ascended to heaven. The Bible says that, **"When he ascended on high, He led captivity captive, and gave gifts to men" (Ephesians 4:8).** You have been given gifts and talents for your use. Discover what you've been given and it will make a way for you.

People must realize that there is something they have which if properly polished and package and served to people, people will in return offer them the money they don't have. The more you think of what you can get from people, the poorer you will become. Even if God wants to bless you with good, He usually would create an opportunity where you can trade what you have (a knowledge, an idea, a gift or talent, a skill or an ability) for the money you don't have. Anytime you chase money directly, money will rather run away from you. The wise man Solomon once said, "He who loves money will not be satisfied with money" (Ecclesiastes 5:10a). The Bible also says that,

> *"It is more blessed to give than to receive". -* **Act 20:35**

Paul once sent Timothy to the church at Philippi simply because Timothy was the only person who at the time had a genuine concern for the welfare of the people. His passion was to see the wellbeing of the people of God. Until you have a genuine desire to see the wellbeing of God's people, or people in general for that matter, you will not succeed in the work God has called you to do. Until what you do for people springs from a genuine desire to see their well-being, you will become a burden instead of a blessing.

> *Until you have a genuine desire to see the wellbeing of God's people, you will not succeed in the work God has called you to do. You will become a burden instead of a blessing.*

You cannot think of your interest alone and succeed in whatever you are doing in this life. If it's always your own benefit that you are concerned about at the expense of others, you will soon find yourself living alone without anybody to share life with. Paul said in the book of Philippians,

> "I hope in the Lord Jesus to send Timothy to you soon, that I also may be cheered when I receive news about you. I have no one else like him, who TAKES A GENUINE INTEREST in your welfare"- **Philippians 2:19-20**

When Paul visited the church at Corinth, he also was more concerned with their welfare rather than his needs. He wanted to make an impact in their lives with the word of God. He wanted to be a blessing to them and not a burden. He was more interested in making a difference in their lives than in what he could benefit from their substance (their wealth). Their well-being was his priority. Their success in life was his first concern. See what he said in the book of Corinthians,

> "How, were you inferior to the other churches, except that I was NEVER A BURDEN TO YOU? Forgive me this wrong. Now I am ready to visit you for the third time, and I will not be A BURDEN TO YOU, because what I want IS NOT YOUR POSSESSIONS BUT YOU. After all, children should not have to save up for their parents, but parents for their children". - **II Corinthians 12:13-14**

Don't visit people because of what you can get from them. If you genuinely don't have anything to offer, whether it be spiritual or physical then please don't visit them. Let your visit to people be because you have something you genuinely want to give. To be more precise, your anointing or gifting as a minister of God or any profession you might be in, is not for your benefit, but for the benefit of others. Since the anointing or gifting is for the people's benefit, grace will flow freely and abundantly when the needs of the people is the only thing occupying your mind. You must therefore crucify the desire to have your needs met and rather stir up the desire to have the needs of others met.

> *You must crucify the desire to have your needs met and rather stir up the desire to have the needs of others met.*

That's why the Bible says that,

> *"Those who belong to Christ Jesus have crucified that sinful nature with its passions and desires".* - **Gal. 5:24**

I want you to remember that, the flow of the anointing, wisdom, counsel, knowledge or whatever ability God has given to you, is proportional to the level of your desire to see other people's lives improve. Your genuine interest in people is the key that allows what is in you to flow to be a blessing to people. Self-centeredness always kills the flow of the graces of God upon our lives.

> *The flow of the anointing is proportional to the level of your desire to see other people's lives improve.*

The only good reason for visiting people or any place is because you have something of value to give or at least for a mutual benefit. Always look for something that you can genuinely give to meet a need in that person's life. Also don't give, be it money, material things, the preaching of the word of God, or prayer etc., with the motive of what you can get back from them. Look up to God as your true source of supply. Let God decide who He uses to bless you. Never demand anything from anyone by your own leadings, let God rather lead you to the right people where you can ask or where God can make the people willingly give to you.

When the Prophet Elijah had need of food in the book of Kings because of the famine at the time, God led him to a woman at a city called Zarephath. God said to him *"I have commanded a widow woman there to sustain you"* (**1 Kings 17: 9-11**). When the man of God got there, he asked of the woman water and a meal because that was where God said he has made provisions. Elijah was not a burden to the widow woman but became a major blessing to her and the family. If it is God leading you, your visit will eventually be a blessing and not a burden to the people concerned.

God does not take to subtract from our lives, but rather he takes what we have to multiply it back unto us, and that's what he did in the life of the widow woman. That is why Jesus took five barley loaves and two fishes from a child and multiplied it to feed five thousand people (John 6:8-12). If indeed it is God leading you, I say it again; it will turn out to be a blessing to the people who are giving to you. But anytime you look to man to meet your need(s) you automatically lose the opportunity to experience the blessings that come from God.

> *If it is God leading you, your visit will be a blessing and not a burden to the people concerned.*

An American preacher - **Mike Murdock** once said *"if you take what God has not given to you, he takes what he has given to you".* Always cross check with the Holy Spirit before you visit anyone. Cross check whether your visit will be a blessing or a burden. Don't let what you will get from people or a place, be the main reason for your movements; let the Holy Spirit lead you. The acid test of your motive for visiting people is when what you can give is the driving force for your visit. Let the leading of the Holy Spirit be the driving force for your visits, so your visits will end up being a blessing and not a burden.

If the Lord is the one leading you, your dignity and honor will be preserve. You will not look like a beggar in front of people. People will not use what they do for you to spite you, because God will cause a blessing to flow into their lives out of their obedience. They will see your coming as a source of blessing to their lives rather than a burden.

> *"Don't let what you will get from a person or a place, be the main reason for your movement".*

THREE KINDS OF VISITATIONS

1. Always Visiting people for the main reason of what you can get from them (Try to avoid this since it makes you look like a beggar - a burden and before time people will start avoiding you).

2. Visiting for the main reason of having something to give to people (This should be your drive because it gives you a reception before people and allow people to open up to you).

3. Visiting for mutual fellowship- i.e. you do not have something in particular to give and likewise, you are not thinking of anything in particular to take. Your motive is for mutual fellowship. (This is good for developing healthy relationships among people).

ANYONE WHO HAS THIS HAS LIFE UNDER CONTROL

The strongest and lasting paddle which can propel anyone through the storms of life to the safest shore is the genuine desire to help people. The genuine desire to help people is the only good reason that has the ability to sustain anyone through the storms of life and still keep him moving forward. It is the foundation for consistency and persistency. Note that, when it is well seated in a person's heart, there is nothing else in this life that can defeat it, not even death. There is no need rushing to move on in life until this single quality of helping people is well in place in your heart. It is the secret to living a fulfilling life. It's enemy is called self-centeredness - living for you.

> *The strongest and lasting paddle which can propel anyone through the storms of life to the safest shore is the genuine desire to help people.*

People who have this quality will overtake those who don't have it on the road to the top. Whiles those who have it are going up, those who don't have it are coming down. **Be Wise!** Your knowledge, your wisdom, your anointing, your money, your time, your strength, your love, your concern are given to you so you can impact the lives of people on this earth. When you have only this one reason for all you do, all will succeed. The chief of all reasons in all you do is helping people with what you do or have. People don't care how much you know until they know how much you care.

> *The genuine desire to help people is the foundation for consistency and persistency in whatever we do in life.*

Rehoboam the son of Solomon, who succeeded his father, wanted advice from the elders who had served his father Solomon as to how to rule over the people. This was the wise counsel the elders gave him though he did not take it and caused him the kingdom. The Bible says that,

> "Then King Rehoboam consulted the elders who had served his father Solomon during his lifetime. "How would you advise me to answer these people?" he asked. They replied, "If today you will be a SERVANT to these people and SERVE them and give them a favorable answer, they will always be your servants." - **1 Kings 12:6-7**

The king was advised to genuinely care for the people. The Elders encouraged him to serve the people, for in serving the people, they would in return be loyal to him always. In the kingdom of God, the one who wants to be the greatest must first be the servant. They advised him to be a servant leader. Servant leadership is the most effective leadership style with people. These elders had been with Solomon and probably also saw the reign of David and had seen how they had served the people especially King David, and the positive effect of such leadership style.

The truth is that, when you learn to serve people genuinely from your heart, they remain forever loyal to you and to all that you do. A genuine interest in people's wellbeing is one of the keys to effective leadership. NOTE: Proverbs 27:23-27; Ezekiel 34:1- know well your people (your flock).

> "The chief of all reasons in all we do should be the genuine desire of helping people with what we have or do".

In his book, **"How to Win Friends and Influence People"**, Dale Carnegie said that, Thousands of salespeople are pounding the pavements today, tired, discouraged and underpaid. Why? Because they are always thinking only of what they want, they don't realize that neither you nor I want to buy anything. If we did, we would go out and buy it. But both of us are eternally interested in solving our problems. And if salespeople can show us how their services or products will help us solve our problems, they won't need to sell to us. We'll buy.

The secret is in your passion to see how well you can make a difference in the lives of people with what you have or do. Never forget that to be genuinely interested in other people is a most important quality for a salesperson to possess – for any person, for that matter. If we want to make friends, let's put ourselves out to do things for other people – things that require time, energy, unselfishness and thoughtfulness.

> *There is no need rushing to move on in life, until this single quality of helping people with what you have or do is well in place in your heart.*

Alfred Adler, the famous Viennese psychologist, wrote a book entitled: *"What life should mean to you".* In that book he says: *"It is the individual who is not interested in his fellow men who has the greatest difficulties in life and provides the*

greatest injury to others. It is from among such individuals that all human failures spring."

Showing a genuine interest in others not only wins friends for you, but may develop in its customers or people a loyalty to your business or company or your ministry. The principle is that, "you must always love your neighbor as yourself" (Mathew 22:39), and "do unto others what you want them to do unto you". If you want others to like you, if you want to develop real friendships, if you want to help others at the same time as you help yourself, keep this principle in mind; "Become genuinely interested in other people". Whatever you want others to do unto you; you must first of all start doing it unto them. The key to fulfilling your glorious destiny is self-sacrifice. You will need to sacrifice self in order to reach out to others.

You must first of all deny yourself, before you can be a blessing to people with what you have. You cannot be preoccupied with yourself (needs) and think that you can still minister to the needs of people. The point is that you cannot eat your cake and still have it. You cannot hold back and still be a blessing. To be a blessing you must let go of yourself in order to serve others.

> *If we want to make friends, let's put ourselves out to do things for other people – things that require time, energy, unselfishness and thoughtfulness.*

You are on the earth as a reward and an answer to some people's problems. For their sake let go of yourself please, so they can receive what God has planned to do for them through you. You are their link to God's blessings. Without you they cannot access the blessings and promises of God for their lives. Thank you for your availability.

The key to fulfilling your glorious destiny is self-sacrifice.

BE CAREFUL OF HUMAN SUPPORT

Choose rather to suffer or work hard with your own hands, than to depend on men to meet your needs; focus all your energies towards the fulfillment of your purpose. Be buried in fulfilling your purpose in life and not in having your needs met. Those who become pre-occupied with their needs, never fulfill their destiny in this life and so become beggars instead. Beggars are always thinking of their needs but givers are always thinking of the needs of others.

Be buried in fulfilling your purpose in life and not in having your needs met.

The Apostle Paul said that,

"But I have used none of these things: neither have I written these things, that it should be so done unto me:

> *for it were better for me to die (suffer), than that any man should make my glorying void". -* **I Corinthians 9:15**

It's better to labor or work hard with your own hands than to trust man for your needs. Choose affliction (hard work) rather than dependence on man to help you get on in life. You must choose rather to face life yourself with confident trust in God, than run around looking for someone to depend on. True help only comes from God, and except God helps you, any kind of help from man will lead to shame or loss. The Bible says that,

> *"For our light affliction which is but for a moment works for us a far more exceeding and eternal weight of glory". -* **II Corinthians 4:1-2**

The book of Hebrews also says that,

> *"Choosing rather to suffer affliction with the people of God, than to enjoy the pleasures of sin for a season; esteeming the reproach of Christ greater riches than the treasures in Egypt: for he had respect unto the recompense of the reward" -* **Hebrews 11:25**

Moses chose to be associated with the people of God and suffer the disfavor of the king of Egypt (Pharaoh), rather than enjoy the riches of Egypt for a moment. Queen Esther chose to suffer with the people of Israel rather than enjoy the delicacies of King Xerxes and forget why she was made queen in the first place. She was ready to face the consequences of her decision to defend the people of God. She was willing to do the purpose of God for her life rather than safeguard her own personal interest.

The Bible says that, Then Esther sent this reply to Mordecai:

> "Go, gather together all the Jews who are in Susa, and fast for me. Do not eat or drink for three days, night or day. I and my maid will fast as you do. When this is done, I will go to the king, even though it is against the law. And if I perish, I perish". - **Esther 4:15-16**

Any human help you employ to solve your challenges will turn to spite you in the end. Human beings will always take credit for what your life has become, if they feel they have contributed in any way to the success of your life. Abraham refused to take things that belonged to the king of Sodom lest he should say he had made him (Abram) rich. He knew God had made a covenant blessing with him and therefore will not need any human help to make him rich. Especially the kind of human help motivated by human interest and not divine purpose. The Bibles says that,

> "And the king of Sodom said unto Abram, Give me the persons, and take the goods to yourself. And Abram said to the King of Sodom, I have lift up mine hand unto the Lord, the most high God, the possessor of heaven and earth, that I will not take from a thread even to a shoelace, and that I will not take anything that is yours, lest you should say, I have made Abram rich." - **Genesis 14:21-23**

People will always want to use the help they give you to manipulate you. Even when they do the wrong thing and you have to rebuke them or correct them, they will make you feel you owe them and so you can't talk to them like that. The Bible says that, "cursed is any man who puts his trust in man and makes flesh his strength, whose heart departs from the Lord" (Jeremiah 17: 5). To trust man is a big snare to one's soul.

> To trust man is a big snare to one's soul.

HUMAN HELP WILL CAUSE YOU TO BE DESPISED IN THE END

God had promised Abraham (the founding father of the Jewish people) a child, but as the promise seemed to delay, Sarah his wife proposed to Abraham her husband that he should sleep with Hagar, one of her maidservants. This proposal was meant to solve their inability to have a child. Sarah felt the time was far gone and if she didn't do something about their situation it might be too late. They wanted a child who would inherit them when they died. So Abraham agreed and slept with Hagar.

The Bible says that, after Hagar had conceived, **"she began to despise Sarah"** (her Madam). She began to disrespect Sarah. Hagar felt she was the "real" woman – the woman carrying a baby and feels more important in the house and thought she could even take Sarah's place. She felt she could not take orders any more from her barren madam. After all, she was the real woman – the woman with a baby. Look at what the Bible says,

> *"And he (Abraham) went in unto Hagar and she conceived: and when she (Hagar) SAW that she had CONCEIVED her mistress was DESPISED in her eyes". -* **Genesis 16:4**

I want you to understand that, the very people you try to use as short cut to solve your problems, will turn against you and despise you. Hagar despised Sarah, because that was not God's solution to their problems. God had promised them a child who will come from the loins of Abraham and the womb of Sarah. Hagar was not part of God's plan and she had no role to play as far as the promised heir of Abraham was concerned. The blessing of the Lord makes one rich and surely it adds no sorrow. Any solution which is from God, which is meant to meet a need in your life, will bring no sorrow with it at the end. The Bible says that, **"Every good gift and every perfect gift truly comes from God" (James 1:17).**

Any human helper motivated by self, will eventually turn to despise you. That is why you need to endure to the end for the salvation of the Lord. These human supports could be from your family members, your relatives, your close friends, colleagues at work etc. Please look up to God for his kind of support or supply. Trust God to use those he's prepared to help you.

> *The very people you use as short cut to solve your problems, will turn against you and despise you – So be careful.*

The book of Proverbs says that,

> *"Do not eat the food of a stingy man; do not crave his delicacies; for he is the kind of man who is always thinking about the cost. Eat and drink, he says to you, but his heart is not with you. You will vomit up the little you have eaten and will have wasted your compliment".* - **Proverbs 23:6-8**

Any help which is not divinely engineered will always bring shame and regrets at the end. People will always make you feel eternally indebted to them. They will always use the help they gave you to manipulate you for their interest. They will always want you to do things their way and if you don't, you are out of their good books. They will use what they have done for you to control your life. Be careful of human help.

After the death of King Saul (the first king of Israel), one of his top military officials called Abner, organized and put one of the sons of Saul, Ish-bosheth as king over the whole tribe of Israel excluding Judah where David later was made king. Abner was a strong and powerful influence during Saul's time. Because Abner organized the enthronement of Ish-bosheth, he made the new king feel indebted to him. The Bible says that one day Abner went and slept with one of Saul's wives which the new king, Ish-bosheth rebuked him for and as a result Abner got offended. Out of his offense, he withdrew his loyalty from the king and then decided to go to David to support him to be king over the whole tribe of Israel. Because he had been rebuked by the new king, the new king was no more in his good books and so he was willing to withdraw his assistance to the king and give it to David (**Read: 2 Samuel 2:8-10; 3:6-11**).

Is this not similar to some of the happenings in our days? There are people who claim to be giving you a helping hand in whatever you are doing, but when you rebuke them or correct them for some wrong doing, they withdraw their support from you. Human help is always self-centered. They are all sinking sand. It is always about themselves and not about you. It is about what they can get out of you. Be careful of human support. If the help is motivated by God there will be no strings attached to it, which could be used later to manipulate you. The book of proverbs we read from above says that, **"eat and drink he says to you, but yet he has an agenda for all of that"**. He is saying to you, "Eat and drink" but he knows it is not for free.

If God does not prepare someone to help you, that help will finally bring pain and regrets because it will not be for free. There is no free lunch outside God. Those that God prepares to bless you will always be excited to be a blessing to you. Because they are prepared by God to help you, the grace to do it will also be upon them. It's a joy and a delight for them to help you and not a burden. Those

God has not ordained to help you, will see any help as a burden and will be thinking of what they can do to get even with you at a later date. Anytime they see you they despise you in their heart because of your circumstances in life. They help you because they feel pity for you and not because they feel a calling by God to help you. Be careful therefore who you go to for help in time of your need. You will need to trust God for his kind of help which comes by his directions or leadings through the Holy Spirit.

Remember a double minded person cannot receive anything good from the Lord. A complete trust is what is needed to attract the hand of God into any bad situation you are in.

> *A complete trust is what is needed to attract the hand of God in any bad situation you are in.*

DEPEND ON THE HOLY SPIRIT LEADINGS

Let me give you an example of what I've been sharing with you. I once traveled to Kumasi in the Ashanti region of Ghana, West Africa and run out of money. I had some friends there I thought of seeing for help. Whiles I was thinking of who to go to for help, the Spirit of God directed me rather to see a friend of my brother-in-law.

I was not acquainted enough with him to have thought of asking him for money, but I obeyed and went to see him in his house. He was very excited to see me and asked of my brother-in-law and his family. We spoke for a while and as we spoke God used me to say things which were of great blessing to him. When I finally asked permission to leave, he went into his bedroom and handed me an envelope containing some money. The point is that, I did not even ask him for any money. God did not even let me tell him my need. God preserved my dignity and honor. The truth is that he has not called us for shame. God will always provide where he directs. Sometimes he will allow you to ask but this time he convicted him to give to me.

> *Divine directions from the Holy Spirit, will always bring divine provisions. Where ever God directs, he always provides.*

He was so delighted to be a blessing to me and even felt what he had given to me was so little; though to me it was more than enough. If I had gone to any of my friends without God's approval they might not even have been in the position to help me. May be they could have given me some money but it might be a burden to them. God's will is for you to be a blessing and not a burden to people. He did not make a mistake in creating you and you are here for a purpose to bless or give something to mankind. God doesn't want you to look like a misfit, no! You have a contribution to make to the people of this earth. He has endowed you with something significant to contribute to the people of this world. Sometimes we don't believe we have something significant to offer the world. But we all matter and that's why we were born, to fix the challenges in the lives of people. What we need is a closer walk with the Spirit of God so we can discover what God has given to us and prepare to serve it to our world. As the Spirit of God directs us and we serve our gifts and talents to our world, his provisions will also come along with it. Divine directions from the Holy Spirit, will always bring divine provisions. Where ever God directs, he provides. Cross check with the Holy Spirit as you seek help from people for beautiful results.

ALWAYS HAVE A GIVING MENTALITY

A giving mentality is a rich mentality. Those who are rich can afford to give because they know that they have more than enough. You don't normally see the poor giving because they "think" they don't have enough. To develop the wealth and abundance mentality is to develop a joyous giving habit.

> *Any liberal soul will be rich and wealthy.*

You must give "knowing" that you have more than enough. If you are a giver then you have an account in heaven and therefore anytime you are in need, and you place a request, supply will come. The bible says that,

> "One man gives freely, yet gains even more; another withholds unduly, but comes to poverty. A generous man will prosper; he who refreshes others will himself be refreshed. - **Proverbs 11:24-25**

As you decide to refresh people through what you have and do, so will you be refreshed by other people. Those who become a blessing to others are massively blessed themselves. Be a part of the success stories of others, for you do not know what God will use them to do in your own life later on. When Joseph was in prison, having been falsely accused of sexual harassment, the Bible says that, he continued to be a blessing to those who had problems in the prison cells. He used his gift of interpreting dreams to interpret the dreams of those who had dreams and ministered to their needs **(Read Genesis 40:1-19)**.

As a result of his genuine desire to help the people around him, the door of great opportunity for him to be made the prime minister of Egypt was opened. **(Read Genesis 41:1-57)**. The same person (the cupbearer) he helped in restoring to his work as Pharaoh's cupbearer was the one God used in promoting him to become the Prime minister of Egypt when the right time came. The point is that, the breakthrough of people that you help to accomplish, will lead to your own breakthroughs later on in life.

The breakthrough of others that you help to achieve will lead to your own breakthroughs later on in life.

The answer to your own breakthroughs lies in the hands of the people around you and as you help them to have their own breakthroughs, so will your own come. If you do not help people to succeed, you will you also not succeed. I repeat: Be a part of the success stories of others, for you do not know what God will use them to do in your own life later on.

> *Be a part of the success stories of others, for you do not know what God will use them to do in your own life later on.*

The book of Ecclesiastes says that,

> *"Sow your seed in the morning, and the evening let not your hand be idle; for you do not know which will succeed, whether this or that, or whether both will do equally well".*
> **- Ecclesiastes 11:6**

Before the people of Israel crossed the Jordan River to go and possess the Promised Land (the land of Canaan), half the tribe of Manasseh, the Reubenites, and the Gadites had already been blessed with their portion on the other side of the Jordan when Moses was still alive. The only condition Moses gave for them to enjoy their portion was to go and help their brethren to also possess their own. The Bible says that,

> *"And Moses said unto them, if the children of Gad and the children of Reuben will pass with you over Jordan, every man armed to battle, before the Lord, and the land shall be subdued before you; then ye shall give the land of Gilead for a possession: But if they will not pass over with you armed, they shall have possessions among you in the land of Canaan".* **- Genesis 32:29-30**

Any time you refuse to help people possess their inheritance, you face the consequence of struggling to cater for yourself. You need faith to believe that indeed your needs are met. You don't need to pray for your needs, pray for the needs of people. You need to believe that God has supplied all your needs in order to focus on the needs of people and on how to help them to possess their own.

The only condition for you to enjoy what God has already provided for you is to help people get their own.

CHAPTER FOUR:
PRINCIPLES

1. The Holy Spirit time is the right time.

2. It is the ability of walking in God's timing that commands success in every adventure we undertake.

3. One major quality of a successful life is the quality of not being easily influenced by natural circumstances.

4. The manifestation of the glory of God is always connected to God's own time.

5. You are not supposed to force yourself to do anything for God, but to be led by the Holy Spirit to do things for God.

6. The man who is easily influenced by natural things will not enjoy the privilege of being influence by spiritual things.

7. How easily you are influenced by natural things is an indication of how weak you are on the inside.

8. Planning coupled with hard work (action) is all you need to start from where you are towards where you want to get to in life.

9   Until what you do for people springs from a genuine desire to see improvement in their wellbeing, you will become a burden instead of a blessing.

10 You must crucify the desire to have your needs met and rather stir up the desire to have the needs of other people met.

11 The flow of the anointing is proportional to the level of your desire to see how well people's lives get better.

12 Never demand anything from anyone, let God rather make people willing to give to you.

13 Don't let what you will get from a person or a place, be the main reason for your visitations.

14 As you contribute to the breakthroughs of others, it will lead to your own breakthrough later on in life.

15 The strongest and lasting paddle which can propel anyone through the storms of life to the safest shore is the genuine desire to help people.

16 The genuine desire to help people is the foundation for consistency and persistency in whatever we do in life.

17. There is no need moving on in life until this single quality of helping people is firmly rooted in your heart; for while those who have it are going up, those who don't have it will be coming down.

18. If you want God's best, do things God's way.

19. Destiny is both a promise and a process. God will show you the promise, and the process must unfold to prepare and position you.

20. Destiny has a time.

CHAPTER FIVE

IF YOU ARE WILLING AND OBEDIENT

"Physical maturity is bound to time. Spiritual maturity is bound to obedience"

- John Bevere -

God is calling His children from their own works into his finished work on the cross, through obedience to the voice of the Holy Spirit by faith. There is rest for the people of God and anyone who enters into this rest will automatically cease from his own works which lead to struggle. **God by His Spirit is helping and leading many into this rest** and it will take our faith in God to get us into it. It is by grace through faith.

Our willingness and obedience to divine directions and instructions is one of the main qualities of a successful walk with God. For The Bible says that,

"The just shall live by faith". **- Romans 1:17 KJV**

Without faith, it will be impossible to please God. We need to please God in order to experience Him and without pleasing God, you cannot possess your inheritance. God is getting all His children back into their divine destinies, where we are only called to dress and to keep what God has already finished for us.

Remember that, in the Garden of Eden everything was finished before God took man and placed him there to **dress it** (work it) and to **keep it** (enjoy it). He was supposed to manage and maintain what God had committed to their hands. Adam was supposed to work the Garden and to take care of it. The book of Genesis says that,

> "And the Lord God took the man, and put him into the Garden of Eden to dress it and to keep it". - **Gen 2:8-15 KJV**

Also, everything was ready before God brought the Israelites into the Promised Land. The Promised Land was a type of the Garden of Eden which represents their place in destiny. The land was exceedingly good, a land flowing with milk and honey. In the book of numbers, the Bible says that,

> "Joshua son of Nun and Caleb son of Jephunney, who were among those who had explored the land, tore their clothes and said to the entire Israelites assembly, "The land we passed through and explored is exceedingly good. If the LORD is pleased with us, he will lead us into that land, a land flowing with milk and honey, and will give it".
> - **Numbers 14:6-8 NIV.**

All that was required was for them to believe that with God it was possible to possess the land regardless of its other occupants in the land. It was theirs as far as God was concerned. In the plan and purpose of God, every person on earth has his or her own destiny. This destiny is already finished and furnished and God wants to lead or is calling every individual child of His into it. Every purpose of God for your life is an exceedingly good one. One that is rich and blessed by God. The bible says that,

> *"For I know the plans I have for you, declare the Lord, "plan to prosper you and not to harm you, plan to give you hope and a future"* - **Jeremiah 29:11 NIV**

Isaiah the Prophet also says,

> *"For the Lord shall comfort Zion: he will comfort all her waste places; and he will make her wilderness like Eden, and her desert like the garden of the Lord; joy and gladness shall be found therein, thanksgiving and the voice of melody".* - **Isaiah 51:3 KJV**

God never planned that His children should be uncertain about and struggle with their lives. The uncertainties and sufferings are due to the fall of man or the disobedience of Adam and Eve, but God through Jesus Christ has saved man from the penalty of sin and has restored man to his original position in God. A position which was to enjoy what God has already prepared for man. We are only to dress it and to keep it for our benefit and his purposes. What we need now is our faith in Christ Jesus which should produce in us a willingness and obedience to follow his instructions and directions. Many are still outside of God's purpose for their lives andHe wants them back into his finished work.

> *Many are still outside the Garden of Eden and God wants them back into his finished work.*

Before the fall, Adam and Eve had everything they needed without struggling for it. God made whatever they needed available in the Garden of Eden. Not even once did they lack anything that pertained to life and godliness. It was after they moved outside of the Garden of Eden (God's finished work), that they began to struggle and to suffer in life. **Many are still outside the Garden of Eden** (that is God's purpose for their lives) and God wants them back into his finished work. One of the reasons so many of God's people today have not taken possession of their inheritance is because they are not being led by the Holy Spirit.

He is saying, "Come let us reason together", for I can change that situation. The main instrument, which will help bring people back into their individual destinies, is their willingness and obedience to the voice of the Holy Spirit – that is, to his instructions and directions.

The main instrument, which can help bring people back to their own Eden, is their willingness and obedience to the Holy Spirit.

The Bible says, **"If ye be willing and obedient, ye shall eat the good of the land" (Isaiah 1:19 KJV)**. The Bible also says that, **"Today if you hear his voice, harden not your heart" (Hebrew 4:7 KJV)**. What instructions or directions have God giving to you to obey? Your prompt obedience to His voice is the key to your victory. **No one can get into his destiny (Promised Land) except the Spirit of God guides him or her.**

Listen, if disobedience to the instructions of God, given to Adam and Eve is what took them out of the Garden of Eden, and then it will take only our **total obedience** to God through the Holy Spirit to fulfil our destinies. The book of Numbers says that,

> *"But my servant Caleb, because he had another spirit with him and hath FOLLOWED ME FULLY, it is he I will bring into the land where into he went; and his seed shall possess it". -* **Numbers 14:24 KJV**

A complete followership of God is what will guarantee your access to your glorious destiny (Garden of Eden). There is the need for you to follow God fully with all your heart, all your soul and all your strength if you must fulfil your destiny completely. A halfhearted approach towards God will not yield any reward.

> *A halfhearted approach towards God will not yield any reward.*

It will take a complete surrender to God and to his ways, if you must fulfil your destiny. Your destiny means a delightful place (a Garden of Eden). God has a delightful place prepared for you to inherit.

WHERE THERE IS A WILL THERE IS A WAY

You see, when people are buffeted by challenges and circumstances, they abandon their life to fate, allowing any kind of junk to come into their lives. They just give up and allow anything to push their life in any direction. They lose control and so they resign their life to whatever comes. One must fight to get his life back on track, where you can control it the way you want it. If you don't fight, you will lose it entirely. "It's not the size of the dog in the fight. It is the size of the fight in the dog" - Mark Twain (An American Author). That's why the Apostle said, **"I have fought a good fight, I have run the race, I have kept the faith and I have finished my course" (2 Timothy 4:7).**

If you don't fight you will never get to your destination. Situations and circumstances plus people will try to push you out of the way from your destination (your destiny). If you allow situations to make you lose control of the steering wheel of your life, then you are sure not to get to your destination for the danger is that you may crush on the way. Your life will then be left to chance and any life left to chance has no chance. You will have to fight to keep control of your life and to move it in the right direction you want and not what circumstances or people want.

> *"Any life left to chance has no chance."*

Life is like a vessel on the sea and without determination to steer it in the desired direction, it will drift and finally drown. See your life as a boat. Without any control or paddles, the boat will drift in any direction with no destination. There must be a deliberate effort to steer it in the direction you desire it to go. If you leave it at the mercy of the wind and the storms, then it has no chance of arriving at a desired destination. What you become is as a result of your God given purpose in life and your willingness to commit to fulfilling it.

YOU ARE NOT PERMITTED TO REMAIN POOR

You are permitted to be born poor but you are not permitted to remain poor. If you remain poor then that's your choice. You cannot choose where you are born, but you can choose where your life finally ends. You can be born in a manger, but you can end up as the saviour of the world. You can be born into a poor family, but you can turn the poverty into riches. It's your choice.

> *You must refuse to remain poor because God is determined to turn your destiny around.*

Jesus was born into a sinful and wicked world, but He saved the world from their sins and gave His righteousness to the world. You must refuse to remain poor because God is determined to turn your destiny around. Though God commanded Israel to leave the surplus (gleanings) of their harvest for the poor, His ultimate design was for everyone to come into their own harvest.

If you remain poor, it's not because God want it so for you, No! It's rather your choice either through laziness or unwillingness or disobedience to follow the will or purpose of God for your life.

> *You are permitted to be born poor but you are not permitted to remain poor.*

Some people prefer to please men instead of obeying God, and so continue to be subject to men. They continue to be servants instead of taking charge of their own destiny. It is not the will of God that your life remain dependent on other people all the time. Your life must depend on the purpose of God for your life. You have a destiny to fulfil and that destiny is bigger and more important than any other man's personal interest.

If we surrender to God and His purpose for our lives, He will lift us up where we belong far above what we can think or imagine. Don't remain poor and totally dependent on the mercy of people for your future. Take your life into your own hands and drive it in the direction the Spirit of God will direct, without fear of the unknown. Remember that somebody's harvest will not be your own harvest. You can only get the surplus from their harvest. God has a harvest for you and therefore you must be ready to work at it.

You must refuse to remain poor because God is determined to turn your destiny around

TAKE CHARGE OF YOUR LIFE

Life should be lived based on **what** and **where** one is going. You don't live your life based on other people's opinions or initiatives. One must have his own motivations and initiatives for living. You must live based on your own goals and dreams. You don't need an overseer; someone to rule over you before you do the things that you know need to be done.

If you wait for someone to come and tell you what you have to do for your own life, then I am sorry you will get nothing accomplished in life. You need to be your own boss, to motivate yourself (encourage yourself) to do what you know needs to be done. You have to have your own motivation for living or else life will become a burden. And to have your own motivation, you must know what you want out of life. Until you know what you want in life, you will get nothing worthwhile out of life. Life gives to you what you sincerely demand of it. If surviving the day is all you expect and plan for, then that is all you are going to get.

> *Until you know what you want in life, you will get nothing substantial out of life.*

The ant, the Bible says, has no overseer or leader or commander yet it gathers its food during summer and stores its food during harvest time (Proverbs 6:6). **Nobody** tells the ant to do **what** it should do and **when** it should do it. It **knows** what needs to be done and does it without any external supervision (influence). The ant is self-motivated, self-sustaining- it needs no applause to keep doing what is the right thing to do. It is motivated by its own sense of purpose and responsibility. It is not told what to do and yet it does the right thing at the right time, and so produces the right results. The ant is not over taken by events, but rather takes control of events. We are admonished to learn from the wisdom and activities of the ant. In short we are being told to take charge of our lives and drive it the way we want it to go.

One must determine to drive his or her life in the direction he or she wants it to go. Don't leave the direction in which your life must go to the opinions and plans or promises of people. People don't even know where you are going and what you are called to do in the first place. People are more interested in what they are doing. They really want to see how they can succeed in their own lives. They have a responsibility to fulfill the plans and goals of their own lives and if you leave your destiny in the hands of people nothing will be done. Hear this, it's very important: "If you don't take charge of your life, you may not get to your destination".

> "If you don't take charge of your life, you may not get to your destination".

BE A GOOD LEADER

A good leader is the one who is self-motivated; has initiatives of his own. One who makes a way where there is no way for others to follow, one who gives hope where there is no hope, one who makes things happen. He does not watch things happen. He changes things and brings life to dead situations. He does not wait for everybody before he does what needs to be done. The point is that, nothing happens when nobody moves. A good leader is the one who moves and gets things moving along with him. He does not give excuses for any situation; he rather looks for solutions to the situations. He's a problem solver.

The Bible says Jesus as our example of a good leader, went about doing good and healing all that were oppressed of the devil (Acts 10: 38). He provided solutions to the people that came to him.

A good leader will fight till he succeeds. He thinks that, there is no reason why he should not succeed. He refuses to accept any situation as a permanent one. He's always determined to improve and change his life. Anyone who easily loses control of his life cannot be a good leader. A good leader will fight to keep his head up high even if he falls into a ditch. He does not easily give up. He knows what is needed to be done and will do anything to get it done.

> *A good leader knows what is needed to be done and will do anything to get it done.*

The word 'excuse' is not in his dictionary or vocabulary. Day and night, he does everything possible to fulfill his dreams and goals. Though getting support from other people is encouraging, great leaders will take their life into their own hands and do what they can. Even without any external support, they will still make the best of every situation they are in (Read Judges 12:3). They do not waste precious time complaining about people disappointing them. They move on in life, doing the best they can to change things. A great leader takes a "nobody" and turns him into "somebody". They will always use what they have to accomplish their goals and dreams. Great leaders oversee themselves. They control themselves. They manage themselves. They are their own commanders. They command themselves to do what is needed to be done when it needs to be done. They demand of themselves to be responsible. They discipline themselves to ensure that they move forward in life.

The point is that, if you judge yourself, then no one can judge you. That is what great leaders do. They do not wait for anybody to judge them, they judge themselves. They make their own corrections and then move on towards their glorious destination.

ATTITUDE IS EVERYTHING

My working life is only about fifteen years old, but with my personal experience with workers, I can say attitude is one of the most damaging hindrances to the personal development of many professionals. It is good to have gifts and talents. And hard work is a much cherished virtue. But hard work and talent cannot get you anywhere if you have a bad attitude towards work. Attitude is key.

Your attitude to work should not be determined by your environment, not even the kind of treatment you get.

According to John C. Maxwell, "People may hear your words, but they feel your attitude." Former US President, Thomas Jefferson, teaches us that: "Nothing can stop the man with the right mental attitude from achieving his goal; nothing on earth can help the man with the wrong mental attitude." For former British Prime Minister, Winston Churchill "Attitude is a little thing that makes a big difference.

"Lou Holtz, a retired American football player and coach, and active sportscaster, author, and motivational speaker once said, "Ability is what you're capable of doing. Motivation determines what you do. Attitude determines how well you do it." The NBA legend, Michael Jordan, always had a positive attitude: "My attitude is that if you push me towards something that you think is a weakness, and then I will turn that perceived weakness into strength."

What I have learnt is that your attitude to work should not be determined by your environment, not even the kind of treatment you get. It is sometimes difficult but it is the best thing to do. The most destructive of all attitudes is the notion that you are only working for your employer and if you don't put in extra effort, it is your employer who loses.

In his letter to the people of Colosse, Apostle Paul advised slaves not to allow how their masters treated them to determine their work attitude: "Slaves, in all things obey those who are your masters on earth, not with external service, as those who merely please men, but with sincerity of heart, fearing the Lord. Whatever you do, do your work heartily, as for the Lord rather than for men, knowing that from the Lord you will receive the reward of the inheritance." (Colossians 3:22-24).

Good attitude determines the difference between winners and losers, and not only hard work, gifts and talents.

Attitude matters. Good attitude determines the difference between winners and losers, and not only hard work and talent. A positive work attitude is a culture that benefits the employee more than the employer and one must not allow external factors to determine their attitude. Always strive to be the best in everything you do, irrespective of your position, or influence or how you are treated. Strive for excellence despite the odds.

If you want posterity to remember you, then in whatever you do, think about what Martin Luther King Jr. once said:

"If it falls your lot to be a street sweeper, sweep streets like Michelangelo painted pictures, sweep streets like Beethoven composed music, sweep streets like Leontyne Price sings before the Metropolitan Opera. Sweep streets like Shakespeare wrote poetry. Sweep streets so well that all the hosts of heaven and earth will have to pause and say: Here lived a great street sweeper who swept his job well. If you can't be a pine at the top of the hill, be a shrub in the valley. Be the best little shrub on the side of the hill. "Be a bush if you can't be a tree. If you can't be a highway, just be a trail. If you can't be a sun, be a star. For it isn't by size that you win or fail. Be the best of whatever you are."

> *For it isn't by size that you win or fail. Be the best of whatever you are.*

CHAPTER FIVE:
PRINCIPLES

1. Many are still outside of God's purpose for their lives and He wants them back into his finished work.

2. The main instrument, which will help bring people back into their individual destinies is people's willingness and obedience to the voice of the Holy Spirit

3. A halfhearted approach towards God will not yield any reward.

4. Any life left to chance has no chance.

5. You are permitted to be born poor but you are not permitted to remain poor.

6. You must refuse to remain poor because God is determined to turn your destiny around.

7. Until you know what you want in life, you will get nothing substantial out of life.

8   "If you don't take charge of your life, you may not get to your destination".

9   A good leader knows what needs to be done and will take whatever steps it requires to get it done – No excuses.

10 Attitude is a little thing that makes a big difference.

11 Good attitude determines the difference between winners and losers, and not only hard work, gift and talent.

12 For it isn't by size that you win or fail. Be the best of whatever you are."

13 Your attitude to work should not be determined by your environment, not even the kind of treatment you get.

14 Physical maturity is bound to time, whiles spiritual maturity is bound to obedience.

www.ingramcontent.com/pod-product-compliance
Lightning Source LLC
Chambersburg PA
CBHW060750050426
42449CB00008B/1340